Contents

Using this guide

Why read this guide?

The purposes of this A-level Literature Guide are to enable you to organise your thoughts and responses to the text, deepen your understanding of key features and aspects and help you to address the particular requirements of examination questions and coursework tasks in order to obtain the best possible grade. It will also prove useful to those of you writing a coursework piece on the text as it provides a number of summaries, lists, analyses and references to help with the content and construction of the assignment.

Note that teachers and examiners are seeking above all else evidence of an *informed personal response to the text*. A guide such as this can help you to understand the text and form your own opinions, and it can suggest areas to think about, but it cannot replace your own ideas and responses as an informed and autonomous reader.

Page references in this guide refer to the Penguin Classics edition of the text, with an introduction and notes by Vivien Jones (2003).

How to make the most of this guide

You may find it useful to read sections of this guide when you need them, rather than reading it from start to finish. For example, you may find it helpful to read the *Contexts* section before you start reading the text, or to read the *Chapter summaries and commentaries* section in conjunction with the text — whether to back up your first reading of it at school or college or to help you revise. The sections relating to the Assessment Objectives will be especially useful in the weeks leading up to the exam.

PHILIP ALLAN

LITERATURE GUIDE

FOR A-LEVEL

PRIDE AND PREJUDICE

JANE AUSTEN

Marian Cox

Series editor: Nicola Onyett

Philip Allan Updates, an imprint of Hodder Education, an Hachette UK company, Market Place, Deddington, Oxfordshire OX15 0SE

Orders

Bookpoint Ltd, 130 Milton Park, Abingdon, Oxfordshire OX14 4SB
tel: 01235 827827
fax: 01235 400401
e-mail: education@bookpoint.co.uk
Lines are open 9.00 a.m.–5.00 p.m., Monday to Saturday, with a 24-hour message answering service. You can also order through the Philip Allan Updates website: www.philipallan.co.uk

© Marian Cox 2010

ISBN 978-1-4441-1623-6

First printed 2010

Impression number 5 4 3 2 1

Year 2014 2013 2012 2011 2010

Printed in Spain

Hachette UK's policy is to use papers that are natural, renewable and recyclable products and made from wood grown in sustainable forests. The logging and manufacturing processes are expected to conform to the environmental regulations of the country of origin.

Cover photo: Keira Knightley and Rosamund Pike in Joe Wright's 2005 film version of *Pride and Prejudice*. © Photos 12/Alamy

P01728

Key elements

Look at the Context boxes to find interesting facts that are relevant to the text.

Context

Be exam-ready

Broaden your thinking about the text by answering the questions in the **Pause for thought** boxes. These help you to consider your own opinions in order to develop your skills of criticism and analysis.

*Pause for **Thought*** ❚❚

Build critical skills

Taking it further boxes suggest poems, films, etc. that provide further background or illuminating parallels to the text.

Taking it **Further** ➤

Where to find out more

Use the Task boxes to develop your understanding of the text and test your knowledge of it. Answers for some of the tasks are given online, and do not forget to look online for further self-tests on the text.

Task

Test yourself

Follow up cross-references to the **Top ten quotations** (see pp. 105–07), where each quotation is accompanied by a commentary that shows why it is important.

❮ Top ten *quotation*

Know your text

Don't forget to go online: **www.philipallan.co.uk/literatureguidesonline** where you can find additional exam responses, a glossary of literary terms, interactive questions, podcasts and much more.

Synopsis

The Bennet family of Longbourn in Hertfordshire, with its five unmarried daughters, is excited by the news that a wealthy young gentleman, Charles Bingley, has rented nearby Netherfield Park. The Bennets attend a ball at which Mr Bingley is present, along with his sisters and his friend Mr Darcy. Although Bingley is taken with the eldest sister, Jane, Darcy refuses to dance with Elizabeth, the second sister, and earns the reputation of being arrogant.

Jane's romance arouses expectations of a proposal, and Darcy finds himself attracted to Elizabeth during the few days she spends at Netherfield looking after Jane, who has caught a chill on her journey there. Bingley's unmarried sister, Caroline — who is herself interested in Darcy — is jealous of Elizabeth and mocks both her and her family. Darcy and Bingley defend them, though Darcy concedes that their lack of wealth and family connections make them poor marriage prospects. Mrs Bennet and the younger girls behave embarrassingly when visiting Jane at Netherfield.

Mr Bennet's cousin, Mr Collins, arrives to stay at Longbourn and admires the house that will one day be his because it is entailed to him. He has been told by his patroness, Lady Catherine de Bourgh, to find a wife, and when Mrs Bennet hints that Jane may soon be engaged, he moves on to Elizabeth. He and the Bennet girls encounter the charming soldier George Wickham, though Darcy snubs him. Wickham tells Elizabeth that although Darcy's father, his own father's employer, had intended to provide for him, Darcy did not honour the agreement. Elizabeth believes his story immediately, although Jane and Miss Bingley both warn her not to. To Elizabeth's dismay, Wickham does not attend the ball given by the Bingleys, and her unhappiness reaches its peak when she finds herself dancing with Darcy and having an awkward conversation about Wickham. At supper, Mrs Bennet discusses the hoped-for union of Bingley and Jane so loudly that Darcy hears.

Mr Collins proposes to Elizabeth, who turns him down against her mother's wishes. A letter arrives for Jane from Miss Bingley, informing her that they are all returning to London and implying that Bingley plans to marry Darcy's sister, Georgiana. Charlotte Lucas agrees to marry Mr Collins. Mrs Bennet's brother and sister-in-law, the Gardiners, come to stay and Mrs Gardiner warns Elizabeth that Wickham's need of money makes him an unsuitable marriage prospect. Jane and the

PHILIP ALLAN LITERATURE GUIDE FOR A-LEVEL

Gardiners depart for London, where Jane calls on Miss Bingley but is treated coldly.

Elizabeth travels with Sir William and Maria Lucas to visit Charlotte in her new marital home at Hunsford Parsonage, adjacent to the mansion of Darcy's aunt, Lady Catherine de Bourgh. Darcy and his cousin Colonel Fitzwilliam come to stay with their aunt at Rosings. Darcy tells Elizabeth that Bingley is unlikely to spend time at Netherfield Park in the future and Colonel Fitzwilliam mentions to her Darcy's claim to have recently saved a friend from an imprudent marriage, so Elizabeth is now certain that Darcy is the agent of her sister's unhappiness. She is resolved to avoid him, but Darcy finds Elizabeth alone at the parsonage and abruptly declares his love for her. His proposal dwells upon her social inferiority and Elizabeth angrily rejects him because of his treatment of Jane and Wickham. The next day Darcy gives her a letter in which he defends himself for breaking up Bingley's romance with Jane by saying that he did not believe her to have been serious, and exposing Wickham as a liar who had attempted to elope with Darcy's sister in the hope of obtaining her fortune. In some confusion Elizabeth leaves Hunsford for home.

Elizabeth tells Jane about Darcy's proposal and the truth about Wickham. They debate whether to expose him publicly, but decide against it. Lydia is invited to spend the summer in Brighton by the wife of Colonel Forster, much to Kitty's chagrin. Mr Bennet refuses Elizabeth's advice that he should forbid her to go.

Elizabeth accompanies the Gardiners on a tour of Derbyshire, which includes Darcy's beautiful home, Pemberley, where the housekeeper describes Darcy as the best of sons, brothers and masters. While they are still in the grounds, Darcy himself suddenly appears, behaves politely, and joins them on their walk. He explains that he has returned early to prepare for guests, which include his sister, whom he would like to present to Elizabeth. The next day, Darcy and Georgiana visit Elizabeth at her inn, followed by Bingley. When Elizabeth and the Gardiners — who perceive that Darcy is in love with their niece — make the return visit, Bingley's sister makes spiteful comments.

Jane writes to tell Elizabeth that Lydia has eloped with Wickham and that as they are not married, Mr Bennet has gone to London to find them. If Wickham does not marry Lydia, the reputations of the entire family will be ruined. Darcy appears and she tells him everything before the Gardiners take Elizabeth home to Longbourn.

Mr Gardiner follows Mr Bennet to London but the search for the couple is unsuccessful, and soon Mr Bennet returns home. Finally, Mr Gardiner

writes to tell him that Wickham and Lydia have been found and that Wickham will marry her if the Bennets will guarantee him a small income. Mr Bennet gladly acquiesces, assuming that the Gardiners have paid Wickham a sizeable amount to get him to agree to the wedding.

Elizabeth realises that her opinion of Darcy has changed so completely that if he were to propose to her again, she would accept, but given Lydia's shameful elopement and the addition of Wickham to the Bennet family, there is now a 'gulf impassable' between them. When describing her wedding, Lydia lets slip that Darcy was there, so Elizabeth writes to Mrs Gardiner asking for an explanation. She replies that it was Darcy who found Lydia and Wickham, and bribed him to marry her, but that he wished to keep this quiet so that the Bennets would not feel obliged to him.

Bingley returns to Netherfield and eventually proposes to Jane. She has learnt that Bingley had no idea that she was in London over the winter because his sisters were determined to keep him away from her. After the engagement, Lady Catherine de Bourgh arrives at Longbourn to inform Elizabeth that she has heard a rumour that Elizabeth and Darcy are planning to marry. She absolutely forbids this, given Elizabeth's low station in life and the tacit engagement of Darcy to her own daughter. Elizabeth conceals her surprise and refuses to promise not to enter into an engagement with him in the future. Lady Catherine leaves, furious and frustrated.

When Darcy and Elizabeth next find themselves alone, Elizabeth thanks him for saving Lydia's good name. Darcy replies that he did so for her sake and that he still loves her. After the two weddings, Bingley purchases an estate near Pemberley, Elizabeth becomes great friends with Georgiana, and Lady Catherine eventually accepts the marriage.

PHILIP ALLAN LITERATURE GUIDE FOR A-LEVEL

Chapter summaries and commentaries

Volume One

Chapter 1

The news that a wealthy young gentleman named Charles Bingley has rented Netherfield Park causes a great stir in the neighbourhood, especially in the Bennet household with its five unmarried daughters. Mrs Bennet insists that their father call on the newcomer immediately. He pretends that he has no intention of doing so.

Commentary: **The first sentence is one of the most famous in English literature. It indicates the author's ironic mode on several levels: it is not 'a truth universally acknowledged', it mocks Mrs Bennet for thinking so, and it draws attention to the unromantic connection between marriage and money. These overriding social themes, both linked by the concept of 'property' and 'fortune', are therefore raised in the very first words by the authorial voice, which will appear at other times to ironic or didactic effect. The characters of Mr and Mrs Bennet, and the nature of their incompatible partnership of 23 years, are economically conveyed by their argument — her nagging and his teasing — and the reader is positioned to be on Mr Bennet's side because of his superior intelligence and sense of humour. Because he prefers Lizzy, and because his wife's favourites are Jane and Lydia, the reader is positioned to like Lizzy too, thus paving the way for her being the novel's main character and narrative persona.**

Typically, Mrs Bennet is the first to speak in the novel. Her husband is reluctant to do so, having more important things to think about than 'his lady's' wittering about Netherfield Park. She is quickly established as a gossip, and someone who is competitive with her neighbours and concerned about the rules of visiting. This alleged conformity to convention will turn out to

*Pause for **Thought*** ⏸

Why do you think Austen opens the novel with such a provocative statement? What is its effect upon the reader?

Typically, Mrs Bennet is the first to speak

be ironic when she later embarrasses and disgraces the family by her vulgar behaviour.

The family composition is conveyed; five daughters were highly undesirable in an age when girls needed dowries to have any hope of finding a husband and when single, eligible bachelors were hard to meet. The plot situation is introduced and it follows that of a classic romance tale; a newcomer is about to enter the locality and will inevitably prove a catalyst in the community, causing changes in behaviour and relationships. This opening chapter conveys much information on the novel's characters, plot, themes and style.

The description of Mrs Bennet as 'a woman of mean understanding, little information, and uncertain temper' is direct and harsh; her self-regard and hypochondria are hinted at here. There is a warning in the judgement of Mr Bennet also, since 'reserve', 'caprice' and sarcasm were not considered acceptable character traits at the time, or indicative of being a responsible parent, as will be proved later. In Jane Austen's fictional world, a character reveals their moral values by the way they speak, and how much speaking they do. All extremes are suspect, and wit is no substitute for wisdom.

Chapter 2

Mr Bennet tells the family that he has been to visit Bingley, and they are overjoyed.

Commentary: **Mr Bennet has enjoyed thwarting his wife's desires by making her believe he has refused to call on Bingley when he intended to do so all along. He has no fortune or property to pass on to his daughters, a serious impediment to their future security, and fully understands the necessity of their all finding husbands. At the time, a female had to be supported first by her father and then by her husband, since she could not work for a living and remain respectable.**

The reader is introduced to, and invited to disapprove of, Mary the would-be intellectual, Kitty the cougher and Lydia the precocious.

Chapter 3

Bingley returns the visit and is invited to dinner shortly afterward, but he is called away to London. When he returns to Netherfield with his two sisters, his brother-in-law, and a friend named Darcy they attend the Meryton ball, which the Bennet sisters attend with their mother. Jane Bennet dances twice with Bingley, who describes her, within Elizabeth's hearing, as 'the most beautiful creature' he has ever beheld. Bingley suggests that Darcy dance with Elizabeth, but Darcy refuses. Elizabeth takes an immediate dislike to Darcy, a dislike shared by the rest of the neighbourhood.

Commentary: **The unreliability of gossip and first impressions is highlighted in this chapter. Darcy is an opposite to his friend Bingley; according to the formula of romances, contrasting character pairs represent extremes, in this case affability versus aloofness. The slight of Elizabeth by Darcy, a blow to her pride, sows in her the seed of prejudice. From this seed grows her negative view of him, her later presuppositions and her willingness to believe ill of Darcy and well of Wickham. He is likewise guilty of both pride (not caring about the impression he is making on the local community or whose feelings he is hurting) and prejudice (assuming country dwellers cannot be taken seriously). They are therefore matched from this first encounter.**

Mrs Bennet's account of the ball uses exaggerated expression (exclamations and superlatives) and shows a preoccupation with gowns that reveal her lack of emotional restraint and her shallow, materialistic priorities.

Chapter 4

Elizabeth realises that Jane has fallen for Bingley and that she likes his haughty sisters. We are told that Darcy finds the inhabitants of Meryton to be lacking in beauty and fashion.

Commentary: **We learn from the conversation between the two elder sisters that they are different in temperament, with Jane always seeing the best in people. We are prepared to dislike the Bingley sisters by Elizabeth's condemnation of them as being 'proud and conceited'. It is also held against them that their family's wealth 'had been acquired by trade'. The *nouveaux riches* were looked down upon by Austen's contemporaries, who only respected 'old money' which was handed down through generations of respectable landed gentry. Bingley's precipitate behaviour in having rented Netherfield Hall and 'the easiness of his temper' are a warning of the likelihood of his doing something foolish in the future.**

*Pause for **Thought***

The novel was originally entitled *First Impressions*. What are your first impressions of Elizabeth and Darcy and on what evidence? Are your impressions manipulated by the way Austen introduces these characters?

*Pause for **Thought***

What is there in the presentation of Darcy and Bingley to suggest that Darcy will become the primary focus of interest?

Taking it **Further**

This first ball sets up the plot for the rest of the book. Look at how the ball is presented in two or more film/television productions (see p. 108 of this guide for a list) and compare how these first interactions between the main characters are presented.

Note the rivalry between Lady Lucas and Mrs Bennet over who should win the love of Bingley, and the women's dependence on hearsay and analysis of social events. They had very little else to do in the rural society of the time than envy and criticise their neighbours.

Chapter 5

The Bennets discuss the ball with their neighbours and friends, the Lucases. They predict that something will come of Bingley's preference for Jane and criticise Darcy's pride.

Commentary: **The Lucas family is offered as comparison to the Bennets. Unlike Mr Bennet, Sir William Lucas has provided well for his family and enjoys a high station in the community. Elizabeth's friend Charlotte is already 27, and described as 'sensible'. To be unmarried by that age means that she is in danger of being left 'on the shelf' and remaining a spinster; not a desirable fate either for her or her family, so we may expect her to accept any offer of marriage which comes along.**

Chapter 6

Bingley continues to court Jane, whom Elizabeth decides is 'in a way to be very much in love', but Charlotte warns Elizabeth that Jane is concealing it too well and that Bingley may lose interest. Darcy is attracted to Elizabeth and listens to her conversations with others. At a party at Lucas Lodge Sir William attempts to persuade Elizabeth and Darcy to dance together, but Elizabeth refuses. Darcy tells Bingley's unmarried sister, who is interested in him herself, that 'Miss Elizabeth Bennet' is now the object of his admiration.

Commentary: **Charlotte will turn out to have observed and spoken wisely, whereas Elizabeth assumes wrongly that everyone is as perceptive as herself. Charlotte's view of marriage is that it is 'entirely a matter of chance', which brings to the fore the question of what makes a good marriage. Elizabeth adopts a teasing, confrontational mode with Darcy to protect herself from further hurt. Caroline Bingley's attack on Mrs Bennet as a future 'charming mother-in-law' makes Darcy begin to worry about his friend's interest in Jane.**

Pause for **Thought**

Pride and Prejudice has been described as 'a novel as much about property as it is about love'. How different would the story have been if the Bennets' property had not been entailed to Mr Collins?

Chapter 7

The fact that Mr Bennet's property is entailed and cannot be inherited by his daughters is explained. His two youngest children, Catherine and Lydia, begin visiting Meryton to flirt with and gossip about the soldiers now stationed there. A note arrives inviting Jane to Netherfield Park for a day. Mrs Bennet sends Jane by horse rather than coach, knowing that it will rain and that Jane will have to spend the night there. As it turns out, Jane is soaked through and falls ill. Elizabeth goes to visit her, on foot through mud. When she arrives with a dirty petticoat and untidy hair she causes quite a stir. Jane insists that her sister stay the night, and the Bingleys consent.

Commentary: **Soldiers are an obvious lure for girls looking for excitement and husbands, but it is to Lydia's and Kitty's shame — 'two of the silliest girls in the country' according to their father — that they make their interest so obvious. A visit to their mother's sister, Mrs Philips, as bad an influence on them as their mother, provides an excuse for them to go to Meryton where the regiment is billeted. A walk to town and a browse in the hat shop is the only outdoor activity allowed to respectable young women; even that is subject to the state of the roads because of their long dresses, which must be protected from rain and mud to avoid, respectively, illness and jeering, as Jane and Elizabeth illustrate.**

A feverish cold was frequently fatal before the discovery of temperature-reducing medicine. The irresponsibility of Mrs Bennet in particular is demonstrated here, as she risks Jane's life to further her matchmaking scheme. She is also the cause of Elizabeth's having to walk three miles, alone, across muddy fields to visit her sick sister, and of her arriving both with 'dirty stockings' and 'a face glowing with the warmth of exercise'. This was a socially contemptible physical state, a statement of abandonment of decorum, in a world where women had to play the doll-like role of drawing-room decorations. Darcy, however, finds Elizabeth even more attractive.

Caroline's letter reveals that she and her sister do not get on, indicating a lack of true family feeling which will soon be applied to her brother as well. The Hursts are another example of a loveless marriage; that Mr Hurst was 'thinking only of his breakfast' shows a lack of proper values.

Chapter 8

While Elizabeth is sitting with Jane, the Bingley sisters make fun of Elizabeth's 'wild' appearance and the Bennets in general. Darcy and Bingley defend them, though Darcy concedes that their lack of wealth and family connections make them poor marriage prospects. When Elizabeth returns to the room, the discussion turns to Darcy's library at his ancestral home of Pemberley, and then to Darcy's opinion of what constitutes an 'accomplished woman'. Elizabeth argues that he is too demanding.

Commentary: **Darcy's growing attraction to Elizabeth is made clear in their sparring dialogue, his defence of her against the sniping Bingley sisters, and a shared interest in libraries and reading, as**

opposed to playing cards. Darcy's sister is mentioned for the first time, and will obviously become significant later in the pairings of the eligible young people.

Context

Chapter 9 introduces the contemporary 'country versus town' debate. Darcy is scathing about the country, describing it as 'confined and unvarying'. Austen was firmly in favour of village life. The Bingley sisters are the main representatives of London in the novel, and their traits are ostentation, shallowness, snobbery, and vice. Darcy is really associated with the country, by virtue of his estate in Derbyshire.

Chapter 9

The next day, Mrs Bennet arrives with Lydia and Kitty to visit Jane. To Elizabeth's dismay, Mrs Bennet tries to convince Bingley to remain at Netherfield and boasts about the locality and her connections with its leading families, causing embarrassment to her family and smirks from the Bingley sisters. Lydia gets Bingley to agree to hold a ball at Netherfield when Jane is recovered.

Commentary: **Mrs Bennet delights in the excuse to visit Netherfield and show off her daughters, and takes the opportunity to put down the rival, Charlotte. She is oblivious to the pain she causes Elizabeth by 'exposing herself' in all her vulgarity, and to her offence against the social graces of modesty and tact. Darcy is scathing about the country, describing it as 'confined and unvarying'. The 'high animal spirits' of the 15-year-old Lydia cause her tactlessly to reveal that balls are more important to her than her sister's recovery.**

Chapter 10

In the evening, Elizabeth observes Miss Bingley piling compliments upon Darcy as he writes to his sister. The conversation turns prophetically to Bingley's impetuous behaviour and an argument over the wisdom of accepting the advice of friends. Elizabeth again refuses to dance with Darcy, which only increases his admiration of her; he considers that 'were it not for the inferiority of her connections, he should be in some danger'. Miss Bingley, jealously observing his attraction, spends the following day making fun of Elizabeth's family, and the idea of it being connected to his.

Commentary: **Darcy's devotion to his sister is shown as he writes her a long letter. Miss Bingley's flattery does not impress Darcy, who makes it clear that he has no time for the deceitfulness of fake humility. The discussion on the subject of how far one should take the advice of one's friends exposes Bingley's carelessness about his decisions and actions; his willingness to 'yield without conviction' is a character fault which shows lack of understanding and harms others. Ironically, Elizabeth is arguing on the side of allowing a friend to have influence; it is one of many instances of her making a wrong choice herself.**

Jane's illness has given Elizabeth and Darcy prolonged exposure to each other's company in an informal setting, which could not otherwise have been managed. When we are told that she 'liked him too little to care for his approbation' we are not convinced, since she has noticed that he is looking at her and has given it some thought. This is an example of the way in which the novel deliberately confuses the viewpoint of Elizabeth with the narrative voice to mislead the reader, as Elizabeth has misled herself about her own feelings. Darcy is now 'bewitched' by Elizabeth and her mixture of 'sweetness and archness' gives her the balanced temperament, avoiding extremes, which was highly regarded in the late eighteenth century. The Bingley sisters, like the two ugly sisters in Cinderella, are jealous and rudely exclude Elizabeth, taking one of Darcy's arms each to lay claim to him. Elizabeth is described as running, rambling and rejoicing, verbs which express her freedom from the social constraints (as represented by the female Bingleys) which Darcy, being intelligent and sensitive, is beginning to question and to see as 'rudeness' and, ironically, as the 'conceit and impertinence' of which Caroline has accused Elizabeth.

Chapter 11

Miss Bingley tries to attract Darcy's attention, first by reading, then by criticising the foolishness of balls and finally by walking about the room. Only when she asks Elizabeth to walk with her, however, does Darcy look up. The two women discuss the possibility of finding something to ridicule in his character.

Commentary: **Darcy refuses to play cards and picks up a book instead, which suggests Elizabeth's influence. Elizabeth teases Darcy about his seriousness and says she dearly loves to laugh, while he admits to being 'too little yielding'. Again the concepts of pride and prejudice are touched upon.**

Chapter 12

Elizabeth and Jane are ready to return home. Mrs Bennet wishes Jane to stay longer with Bingley, so refuses to send the carriage. Elizabeth, anxious to be away, insists on borrowing Bingley's carriage and she and her sister leave Netherfield. Darcy is glad to see them go, as he is attracted to Elizabeth but considers her unsuitable as a prospective wife.

Commentary: **Mrs Bennet fails to welcome her daughters home, and while their father is pleased to see them this is largely**

because he was so bored by the trivial or tedious conversation of their mother and sisters.

Chapter 13

Mr Bennet reads out Mr Collins's letter mockingly. Mr Collins arrives at Longbourn and apologises insincerely for being entitled to it, while simultaneously admiring the house that will one day be his.

Commentary: **Mr Collins's letter is suitably formal but also wordy and smug. Mr Bennet agrees with Elizabeth that he cannot be 'a sensible man' and predicts rightly that Mr Collins will provide amusement, the pursuit of which is Mr Bennet's main goal in life. This pompous comic figure, with the serious moral defects of hypocrisy, sycophancy, egotism and insensitivity, is also an agent for Lady Catherine, Darcy's aunt.**

Chapter 14

Mr Collins praises Lady Catherine de Bourgh and her daughter. After the meal, he refuses to read from a novel and takes up a book of sermons instead. Lydia becomes so bored that she interrupts his reading with more gossip about the soldiers. Mr Collins is offended and abandons the reading.

Commentary: **The opening passage of the chapter is a good example of what is termed 'free indirect speech', a classic feature of Austen's narrative style (see p. 67 of this guide). Although in the mode of third person reportage, the passage uses the vocabulary and sentence structures of Mr Collins himself to convey his many character faults.**

While Austen satirises Mr Collins and his choice of reading matter, she also emphasises Lydia's empty-headedness. For a clergyman, Collins is surprisingly keen on board and card games, as will be confirmed later.

Chapter 15

Mr Collins has been told by his patroness to marry, and when Mrs Bennet hints that Jane may soon be engaged, he fixes his attention on Elizabeth. He accompanies the sisters to Meryton, where they encounter one of Lydia's officer friends, Mr Denny. Denny introduces his friend George Wickham, who has just joined the militia, and the young women find him charming. While they converse, Darcy and Bingley pass by and Elizabeth notices that Wickham and Darcy are extremely cold to each other. Darcy and Bingley depart, and the

Context

The original form of the novel, called *First Impressions*, was epistolary. The letters which remain serve to convey character as well as plot. See 'Epistolary novels', pp. 56–57 of this guide.

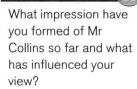

Pause for **Thought**

What impression have you formed of Mr Collins so far and what has influenced your view?

company pays a visit to Mrs Philips, who invites the Bennets and Mr
Collins to dine at her house the following evening. The girls persuade
her to invite Wickham as well.

Commentary: **It is humorous but reflects badly on Mr Collins that
he is following his patroness's command in seeking a wife, and
that he is not particular as to who it is. He is able to change the
object of his intentions 'while Mrs Bennet was stirring the fire'.
He is summed up critically and paradoxically by the author as
'a mixture of pride and obsequiousness, self-importance and
humility'.**

Chapter 16

At the Philips' dinner party, Wickham is the centre of attention; he tells
Elizabeth that he had planned on entering the ministry, rather than the
militia, but was unable to do so because he lacked money. He says that
although Darcy's father had intended to provide for him, Darcy used
a loophole in the will to keep the money for himself. Elizabeth, who
instinctively likes and trusts Wickham, accepts his story immediately.
Wickham also tells her that Darcy is Lady Catherine de Bourgh's
nephew, and describes the aunt as 'dictatorial and insolent'. Elizabeth's
antipathy to Darcy has been strengthened.

Commentary: **Elizabeth falls into the trap of judging Wickham
by first impressions, having been predisposed to find him
attractive and amiable by her knowledge that Darcy dislikes
him. He charms her by not joining in the card games, giving
her his undivided attention and reinforcing her own prejudices
by holding forth about Darcy's pride. Discovering that he has
apparently been ill-treated by Darcy clinches her contempt
for the latter and her liking for Wickham. She is seduced by
his flattery into ignoring the impropriety of the personal
information he is giving to someone he has only just met.
'Elizabeth went away with her head full of him', which sets
up the reader's expectation that something will come of this
meeting and conversation.**

Chapter 17

Elizabeth tells Jane what she has learned from Wickham. Jane defends
Darcy, saying that there is probably a misunderstanding between the
two men, but Elizabeth will have none of it. When Bingley invites the
neighbourhood to a ball the following Tuesday, she looks forward to
seeing Wickham. Unfortunately, she is forced to promise the first two
dances to Mr Collins.

*Pause for **Thought***

Wickham's introduction
complicates the plot,
not only because there
is obviously a mystery
to be solved between
him and Darcy, but
because another
eligible young male,
and potential rival,
has been added to
the marriage stakes.
Consider how Austen
presents Wickham to
mislead the reader
as to the romantic
matches which are
likely to occur.

Context

Judging from
Wickham's conversation,
the events of the novel
take place at the height
of the Napoleonic Wars.
Yet this is hard for the
reader to imagine. For
more information see
'War and revolution'
(p. 82 of this guide) and
for the social role of
officers see pp. 86–87
in the *Contexts* section.

Commentary: **Jane is right in thinking that it is unlikely Darcy would have broken a promise or the obligation of a gentleman to look after the family of a loyal retainer, and Elizabeth wrong to trust Wickham because of his looks. Mr Collins is as keen on dancing as he is on gambling, it is revealed, though neither activity was deemed fitting for a man of the church.**

Chapter 18

Much to Elizabeth's dismay, Wickham does not attend the ball. Denny tells Elizabeth and Lydia that Darcy's presence keeps Wickham away from Netherfield. Elizabeth's unhappiness increases during two clumsy dances with Mr Collins and reaches its peak when she finds herself dancing with Darcy. Their conversation is awkward, especially when she mentions Wickham, a subject Darcy clearly wishes to avoid.

At the end of the dance, Elizabeth encounters Miss Bingley, who warns her not to trust Wickham. Elizabeth assumes that Bingley's sister is only being spiteful, however, and ignores the warning. Jane then tells her sister that she has asked Bingley for information about Wickham, but everything Bingley knows about the officer comes from Darcy and is therefore (in Elizabeth's mind) suspect.

Keira Knightley as Elizabeth and Matthew Macfadyen as Darcy in the 2005 film

Mr Collins, meanwhile, realises that Darcy is related to his patroness, Lady Catherine, and insists on introducing himself, which is greeted with contempt by Darcy. At supper, Mrs Bennet discusses the hoped-for union of Bingley and Jane so loudly that Darcy hears. Mary performs a terrible song for the company, and Mr Collins delivers a speech of absurd pomposity. Elizabeth feels that her family has completely embarrassed itself.

Commentary: **It is ironic that Elizabeth holds Bingley's 'blind partiality' against him in relation to his friend, when she is guilty of exactly the same offence and 'determined to hate' Darcy. Her pique at finding Wickham absent adds to her grievances against Darcy. In ignoring warnings from both Charlotte and Miss Bingley we see how deep her prejudice and belief in her own judgement are, and become aware that she is therefore heading for a fall.**

Mr Collins deserves to be snubbed by Darcy, as it was considered impertinent to approach someone to whom you had not been introduced. The reader can appreciate Darcy's concern for his friend marrying into the Bennet family, which would include Mr Collins, after the collective pretension and vulgarity exhibited here. Notice how economically Austen sketches character with just a phrase at the end of this chapter. Lydia's 'Lord, how tired I am!' accompanied by a 'violent yawn' conveys her offence against propriety in an exclamation, an inappropriate invocation of the deity, a reference to her own physical state of no interest to anyone else and finally the vision of her open mouth in the rude yawn; the extremity of her behaviour is conveyed by the word 'violent'.

Though it was not unusual for parents to have favourite children at the time, it still comes as a shock to a modern reader that Elizabeth is 'the least dear to her [Mrs Bennet] of all her children' and makes us doubt her judgement and fitness to be a mother.

Chapter 19

Mr Collins proposes marriage to Elizabeth, assuming that she will be overjoyed. She turns him down in a spirited fashion.

Commentary: **This splendidly ironic and humorous chapter brings into collision the totally different world views of Elizabeth and Collins, and in particular the proto-feminist and the patriarchal attitudes to marriage.**

Chapter 20

Mrs Bennet is furious that Elizabeth has turned Mr Collins down and tries in vain to get her husband to order Elizabeth to marry him. Mr Colllins withdraws his suit, his pride having been hurt.

Commentary: **Mr Bennet's support of Elizabeth wins the reader's admiration. It is to be remembered, however, that finding husbands is one of his responsibilities as the father of five daughters with no financial independence, and therefore a topic to be taken seriously rather than used as an occasion to frustrate his wife and make witticisms.**

Chapter 21

Elizabeth encounters Wickham in Meryton. He apologises for his absence from the ball and walks her home, where Elizabeth introduces

---

Pause for ***Thought***

Chapter 19 reveals a great deal about Elizabeth's character, ideas and independence of mind. Does it cause you to revise your impression of her?

TASK **2**

Mr Collins's proposal is one of Austen's great comic set pieces. Look at how it is presented in two or three screen versions (see *Taking it further*, p. 108 of this guide), and suggest how you would handle it if you were directing a film version.

Context

The importance of marriage for a girl in Elizabeth's position is discussed in the section 'Social and cultural context' (pp. 85–86 of this guide).

him to her parents. That same day, a letter arrives for Jane from Miss Bingley, informing her that Bingley and his party are returning to London indefinitely and implying that Bingley plans to marry Darcy's sister, Georgiana. Elizabeth comforts Jane, telling her that this turn of events is all Miss Bingley's doing, not her brother's, and that Bingley will return to Netherfield.

Commentary: **The cowardly letter from Miss Bingley is devastating for Jane, but she is too well-mannered to allow it to show and retreats to the bedroom she shares with Elizabeth. Jane reveals her naivety in believing that Miss Bingley is incapable of deceit, and Elizabeth her prejudice against her in not suspecting that anyone else is to blame.**

Context

The pressure upon women to capture a husband is made clear by Charlotte's scheming to win Mr Collins; although she knows him to be 'neither sensible nor agreeable' she accepts him 'solely from the pure and disinterested desire of an establishment' and to relieve her family of financial worry. See the section on 'Marriage', pp. 85–87 of this guide.

Chapter 22

Charlotte informs Elizabeth that she has accepted a proposal from Mr Collins. Elizabeth is shocked, despite Charlotte's insistence that the match is the best for which she could hope at her age.

Commentary: **The reader can see both sides of the argument here and may perhaps think Elizabeth is being harsh in condemning her best friend for having sacrificed 'better feeling to worldly advantage'. We must bear in mind that although we approve of Elizabeth's own assertion of independence and romantic refusal to contemplate a loveless marriage, she is taking a risk for someone in her position in turning down a suitor — as Mr Collins tactlessly pointed out in Chapter 19 — and being undutiful in causing anxiety to her mother. Nevertheless, we appreciate that Mr Collins could not make anyone a tolerable husband.**

TASK 3

This is the end of the first volume of the novel. Imagine that you have not read any further than this, and consider, on the evidence you have been presented with so far, what is likely to happen to Elizabeth and Jane Bennet.

Chapter 23

Mrs Bennet is furious to learn from Sir William that Charlotte will be the future mistress of Longbourn after Mr Bennet's death. As time goes by with no word from Bingley, Jane's marriage prospects begin to fade. Mr Collins returns for another stay at Longbourn.

Commentary: **The first volume ends at a low point for the Bennet family, with no marriage prospect for any of the five girls despite Mrs Bennet's great hopes at the outset of the novel. The marriage and departure of Elizabeth's best friend Charlotte is imminent and Netherfield Hall is unoccupied once more.**

[End of Volume One]

Volume Two

Chapter 24

Miss Bingley writes to Jane praising the beauty and charm of Darcy's sister and confirming that Bingley will remain in London all winter. Elizabeth is very upset on her sister's behalf and complains to Jane that people lack 'merit or sense', referring to both Bingley for abandoning Jane and to Charlotte for agreeing to marry Mr Collins.

Commentary: **Elizabeth's concern for her tolerant, suffering sister is to her credit and in marked contrast to the insensitive handling of the heartbroken Jane by her mother and the cruel comment by her father. The absence of the Bingleys and Darcy, now believed by everyone except Jane to be 'the worst of men', allows Wickham to get a foothold in the affections of the community.**

Chapter 25

Mrs Bennet's brother and sister-in-law, the Gardiners, come to stay for Christmas. Sympathising with Jane, they invite her to accompany them back to London in the New Year, hoping that a change of scenery will raise her spirits. Mrs Gardiner is alarmed by Elizabeth's and Wickham's decided preference for each other, knowing that Wickham must be looking to marry a woman with a fortune.

Commentary: **The Gardiners are superior in character and education to Mrs Bennet, and prove that people who live 'by trade' can be well bred and respectable despite social prejudice to the contrary. Mrs Gardiner's sensitivity, compassion and genuine concern for her nieces contrasts with Mrs Bennet's greater interest in rivalry with the Lucases and the latest London fashion of 'long sleeves'. Coincidentally, Mrs Gardiner knows Pemberley and therefore something of Wickham's background, but though otherwise a fair and sensible woman, she recollects hearing it said in Derbyshire that Darcy as a boy was 'proud' and 'ill-natured'. This again shows how dangerous gossip was at a time when reputation particularly mattered in society.**

Chapter 26

Mrs Gardiner warns Elizabeth that Wickham's need of money makes a marriage between them impossible. After Jane and the Gardiners depart for London, Mr Collins returns for his wedding and Elizabeth promises to visit Charlotte in Kent after her marriage. Jane's letters from London recount how she called on Miss Bingley and how the latter was cold to

her, visiting her only briefly in return. Jane believes that Bingley's sister views her as an obstacle to her brother's marrying Georgiana Darcy (a match which would help Miss Bingley to pursue her own cause of capturing Darcy) and that the Bingleys will never return to Netherfield. Elizabeth admits to Mrs Gardiner that Wickham has turned his attentions to a Miss King, a recent beneficiary of £10,000.

Commentary: **That Mr Bennet favours Wickham because his company is congenial shows an error of judgement on his part as well as being an influence on Elizabeth's, since she is always trying to please her father, the parent who appreciates her and the one she most resembles. Jane finally admits that Miss Bingley has ill-used her, but still tries to make excuses for her. Elizabeth forgives in Wickham what she cannot in her friend — seeking to marry for money — thus revealing inconsistency in her principles and unsound judgement, which varies according to how 'amiable and pleasing' the individual being judged is.**

Chapter 27

Elizabeth travels with Sir William and Maria Lucas to visit Charlotte in her new home at Hunsford Parsonage. On the way, they spend a night in London with Jane and the Gardiners. Elizabeth and her aunt speak about Wickham's attempts to win over Miss King; Mrs Gardiner is critical of his mercenary attitude but Elizabeth defends his prudence in desiring to marry for money. Before Elizabeth leaves London, the Gardiners invite her to accompany them on a tour of the north of England, and she gratefully accepts.

Commentary: **Typically, Elizabeth finds the company of the boastful Sir William and the 'empty-headed' Maria tedious. She is generally dejected and in need of the change of scene her discerning aunt offers her. Elizabeth cannot, however, resist satirising the rapturous, incoherent reports typical of the travel-writing genre at the time.**

Chapter 28

When Elizabeth arrives at Hunsford she is greeted enthusiastically and Mr Collins shows off his house. They are invited to dine at Rosings.

Commentary: **Elizabeth marvels at how resigned Charlotte is to her humdrum existence as a parson's wife, condescended to by Lady Catherine and required to dine at Rosings twice a week. She is trapped, by her husband's profession, into a limited round of domestic chores and social obligations.**

Pause for **Thought** ▌▌

Do you think Austen really shares the conventional view about the necessity of marriage for women without an income (see 'Social and cultural context', pp. 85–86 of this guide)? Is Charlotte really resigned to her fate? What does Elizabeth really think about Charlotte's decision and life?

Chapter 29

Rosings Park overawes everyone but Elizabeth with its pretentious grandeur. At dinner, Lady Catherine dominates the conversation and finds fault with the upbringing of the Bennet girls.

Commentary: **The patronising behaviour of her hostess does not intimidate Elizabeth, who finds Lady Catherine impertinent and as unpleasant as Wickham has alleged. Her spirited defence of her family's unconventional views on governesses and the allowing 'out' of daughters foreshadows the later battle of wills between them. Lady Catherine is the object of Austen's satire through comments such as that she would 'determine what weather they were to have on the morrow'.**

Chapter 30

Sir William departs after a week, satisfied that Charlotte is well established and contented. Darcy and his cousin Colonel Fitzwilliam visit their aunt at Rosings. When Mr Collins pays his respects, the two men accompany him back to his parsonage and visit Elizabeth and Charlotte briefly.

Commentary: **Elizabeth has learned that Darcy is destined to marry his cousin Anne. She finds the Colonel very pleasant, and so another potential love interest is introduced for her. She cannot resist trying to make Darcy uncomfortable by asking him whether he has run into Jane in London.**

Chapter 31

Another invitation to Rosings follows, and Colonel Fitzwilliam pays special attention to Elizabeth during the dinner. After the meal she plays the piano and makes fun of Darcy, informing Colonel Fitzwilliam of his behaviour at the Meryton ball, when he refused to dance with her.

Commentary: **Darcy engages in banter with Elizabeth, but she interprets this as his desire to escape from conversation with his ill-bred and overbearing aunt. The reader's attitude to Darcy softens when we hear his admission that he finds it difficult to talk to strangers.**

Chapter 32

Darcy visits the parsonage and finds Elizabeth alone. He tells her that Bingley is unlikely to spend much of his time at Netherfield Park in the future. The rest of their conversation is awkward, and when Darcy

---

*Pause for **Thought***

Why does Darcy seem more pleasant in Kent than he did in Hertfordshire? Is it because he is no longer being compared with the affable Bingley, but rather with the ill-bred Lady Catherine and the obsequious Collins? However, the Colonel's more relaxed manner disadvantages Darcy in Elizabeth's eyes.

TASK 4

Imagine you are Elizabeth. Write a letter to a friend describing the meeting with Darcy in Chapter 32. Write in Elizabeth's voice, building on her character and capturing aspects of Austen's form, structure and language. Write a brief commentary to accompany your new text which explains how and where you have tried to reflect the original novel.

TASK 5

Make a list of all the women who attempt to match-make in the novel, with the couplings they propose.

Pause for **Thought**

This is a key episode in helping the reader to re-evaluate Darcy. What opinion do you form of his character from this encounter? Does Elizabeth behave any better than Darcy does?

departs Charlotte declares that he must be in love with Elizabeth or he would never have called in such an odd manner.

Commentary: **Once again Charlotte's perception is more accurate than Elizabeth's, whose judgement is distorted by prejudice. Charlotte's attempted matchmaking reveals the main preoccupation for bored married women at the time.**

Chapter 33

Colonel Fitzwilliam mentions that Darcy claims to have recently saved a friend from an imprudent marriage. Elizabeth is certain that Darcy ruined Jane's prospects with Bingley and refuses to go to Rosings, in order to avoid him.

Commentary: **Darcy has been deliberately waylaying Elizabeth on her walks, and has deferred his departure from Rosings, which makes his feelings clear to the reader, if not to Elizabeth. It seems most unlikely that Darcy will ever be forgiven for the pain he has caused Jane and ironic that he would be able to overcome his abhorrence of 'the inconveniences of a most imprudent marriage' on his own account.**

Chapter 34

Darcy finds Elizabeth alone at the parsonage and abruptly declares his love for her. His proposal of marriage dwells upon her social inferiority, and Elizabeth's initially polite rejection turns into angry condemnation when he admits that he interfered in the Jane/Bingley relationship. She then repeats Wickham's accusations and declares that Darcy is proud and selfish, and that marriage to him would be unthinkable. Darcy grimly departs.

Commentary: **This chapter is the climax of the seemingly ill-fated relationship between arrogant rich man and spirited poor girl, and the reader must fear that the clashes of pride and prejudice are too serious to be overcome, while also knowing that, in a romantic comedy, a resolution must be found. Both Elizabeth and Darcy are equally to blame for the unsuccessful proposal, as one of the accusations Elizabeth makes is true (Bingley) and the other is false (Wickham); they are also both provocative, Darcy in pointing out the inferiority of the Bennet family and Elizabeth in telling Darcy that his behaviour is not that of a gentleman. Darcy has made the same gross error as the despised Mr Collins in assuming Elizabeth would consent to his proposal.**

Chapter 35

The following day Elizabeth takes a walk and Darcy gives her a letter in which he tries to defend himself for breaking up Bingley's romance with Jane, in order to spare his friend social embarrassment, by saying that he did not believe her to have been sufficiently involved to be heartbroken. In relation to Wickham, Darcy states that he did provide for him after his father's death but that Wickham attempted to elope with Darcy's sister, Georgiana, to obtain her fortune.

Commentary: **This letter gives us Darcy's perspective and fills in plot strands in a way which has not been possible before. There is now no doubt that he is an honourable man, if sometimes misguided, and the reader is likely to feel that Elizabeth's prejudice has led us to judge him too severely. There is frequent mention of the palings and gates of Rosings Park that symbolise the class barrier between the two protagonists.**

Chapter 36

Elizabeth is stunned by these revelations and although she dismisses Darcy's excuse for his influence over Bingley, his account of Wickham's behaviour causes her to think again and see that she was probably wrong to trust him. Her feelings toward Darcy are now in a state of flux.

Commentary: **This is an epiphany (a sudden revelation) for Elizabeth as she faces up to the need to see things as they really are. She has received and ignored many warnings, thinking she knew better; this is the fall to which her own pride has led her. A principle of ancient Greek philosophy was that one should 'Know thyself'; Elizabeth has not done so until this moment.**

Chapter 37

Darcy and Colonel Fitzwilliam depart from Rosings. Elizabeth informs Lady Catherine that she too must leave, despite the latter's insistence that she stay another two weeks.

Commentary: **Elizabeth accepts that her parents are irresponsible and her two younger sisters 'ignorant, idle, and vain'; but she does not regret refusing Darcy while she still blames him for injuring Jane's prospects. However, she thinks about him endlessly.**

Chapter 38

Elizabeth and Maria travel to the Gardiners' house in London to meet up with Jane.

Pause for *Thought*

Why does Austen choose a letter to present a revised view of Darcy? How else could this have been achieved?

TASK 6

Imagine Darcy explaining to Bingley what has happened with Elizabeth: transform his letter into a dialogue between the two, preserving aspects of his idiom.

Context

A two-month stay was the norm at the time. Slow and uncomfortable travel by horse-drawn carriages on poor roads made visits something to extend whenever possible, and hosts could take offence at an early departure. See 'Country life', p. 89 of this guide.

Commentary: **Although Elizabeth has much to tell Jane it is impossible for the sisters to get together for a quiet talk alone. Though suffering in silence was regarded as a virtue, the lack of privacy and opportunity for necessary communication encouraged secrecy, though this is disapproved of and usually leads to damaged relationships and social disaster in Austen's work.**

Chapter 39

The three girls return home, after being met by Kitty and Lydia in their father's coach. Lydia is full of the news that the regiment is being sent to Brighton for the summer, and that Wickham is no longer interested in Miss King. Mr and Mrs Bennet welcome their daughters home, and the Lucases come for dinner. Lydia has a 'delicious scheme' to persuade her parents to let her go to Brighton too.

Commentary: **Lydia and Kitty are indiscreet and feckless, spending money on bonnets they do not even like and ogling young men. Lydia's voice dominates this chapter, in which she is free from all restraint; her loud utterances are riddled with improper language, and betray an obsession with clothes and husband-chasing. There is a strong hint here that she intends to marry as soon as possible; this is a shocking ambition as the youngest of five sisters, symbolised by the incident she recounts of dressing up in someone else's clothes, and making a spectacle of herself by travelling with the coach blinds open.**

Chapter 40

Elizabeth tells Jane about Darcy's proposal and the truth about Wickham. They debate whether to expose Wickham publicly, ultimately deciding against it. Meanwhile, Mrs Bennet continues to bemoan the loss of Bingley as a husband for Jane, and the prospect of Charlotte and Mr Collins being the future owners of Longbourn.

Commentary: **The Shakespearean theme of appearance versus reality is dwelt upon in the context of the Darcy/Wickham conundrum, of whom 'One has got all the goodness, and the other all the appearance of it.' First impressions are indeed deceptive, and Elizabeth admits that her desire to be considered witty and 'uncommonly clever' took precedence over rational judgement, proving her to be her father's daughter. Jane supports Elizabeth's decision not to let Wickham's villainy become generally known, which turns out to be another mistake. It seems odd to a modern reader that Elizabeth does not share**

---

*Pause for **Thought***

Brighton, like London, symbolises moral danger in Austen's work. Do you think that Mr Bennet values the peace of his library above the moral welfare of his daughters and will be persuaded?

with Jane what she has learned about Bingley, but sparing one's loved ones pain was a high moral imperative in Austen's time.

Chapter 41

Lydia is invited to spend the summer in Brighton by the wife of Colonel Forster, much to Kitty's chagrin. Mr Bennet refuses Elizabeth's advice that he should forbid her to go, since he assumes that the colonel of the regiment will keep her out of trouble. Elizabeth sees Wickham once more before his regiment departs, and they discuss Darcy in a guarded manner.

Commentary: **Mr Bennet is in severe dereliction of his paternal duty in allowing Lydia to go off to Brighton, and in being flippant about Elizabeth's genuine concern about Lydia's 'wild volatility' and the 'general evils' she creates because of her 'rage for admiration'. Elizabeth's impassioned and condemnatory plea to her father falls on deaf ears.**

*Pause for **Thought***

Is Mr Bennet right to think that Colonel Forster can be expected to take responsibility for Lydia?

Chapter 42

Lydia departs for Brighton and Elizabeth accompanies the Gardiners on a tour of Derbyshire, agreeing to visit Darcy's estate only when she is assured that he is not in residence.

Commentary: **The chapter opens with a warning of the dangers of an unsuitable marriage and an admission of the failures of Mr Bennet who, because of his wife's 'weak understanding and illiberal mind' is guilty of 'continual breach of conjugal obligation and decorum' and failure to protect the 'respectability of his daughters'. We know that only Darcy is Elizabeth's perfect match, and the reader is fully expecting a meeting between them on his home ground — otherwise why the last-minute change of itinerary from the Lakes to Derbyshire?**

[End of Volume Two]

*Pause for **Thought***

Volume Two ends on a cliff-hanger. How will Darcy and Elizabeth behave towards each other, given the embarrassment of their last encounter? How might the power of place ('delightful grounds') effect a change in perception and even character as Austen moves them towards one another?

Volume Three

Chapter 43

Elizabeth tours Pemberley with the Gardiners, imagining what it would be like to be mistress there. The housekeeper shows them portraits of Darcy and Wickham and relates that Darcy, in his youth, was 'the sweetest, most generous-hearted boy in the world', and that he is still the kindest of masters. While they are still in the grounds, Darcy himself

Jennifer Ehle as Lizzie and Colin Firth as Darcy after his swim in the lake in the 1995 film

TASK 7

The meeting at Pemberley is a key turning point in the novel. Compare two screen versions of it (see p. 108), then compare them with the famous scene in the 1995 version where Colin Firth's Darcy is seen emerging from the lake in a wet shirt. Do you think this image is a valid interpretation of the text?

Commentary: **As so often in Austen, the house is symbolic of its owner, and the description of tasteful, elegant Pemberley, both inside and out, is allegorical. The housekeeper's account of Darcy, as someone who has known him intimately since he was a child, is objective and corrects the biased opinions of him expressed so far. His devotion to his sister, employees, and the local poor affirm his moral goodness, and another epiphanic moment for Elizabeth occurs while looking at his portrait. Since their last painful meeting he has had time for reflection, and is no longer proud but civil.**

Chapter 44

Darcy and his sister visit Elizabeth at the inn, followed by Bingley. Elizabeth and the Gardiners, who perceive that Darcy is in love with their niece, are invited to dine at Pemberley.

Commentary: **It is difficult to imagine nowadays the honour it bestowed on someone to wish to introduce to them one's dearest relatives, and the imperative of the earliest possible return of a visit if a compliment was to be paid. Georgiana's shyness, misinterpreted by some locals as pride, throws more light on her brother's allegedly haughty reserve. Her contrast with Lydia Bennet, who is of similar age, is meant to be absolute. Darcy's attempt to be amiable to the Gardiners redeems his earlier stand-offishness at Longbourn, and shows how much he has taken Elizabeth's reprimand to heart and wishes to please her now that he has been given another chance. We learn that Wickham left debts behind him (which Darcy paid) when he quit the county, which foreshadows future events. The turning point in the relationship has been reached now that Elizabeth feels gratitude to Darcy.**

Everett Collection/Rex Features

Chapter 45

Elizabeth and Mrs Gardiner visit Pemberley to call on Miss Darcy. Bingley's sisters are both present and, when Darcy enters the room. Miss Bingley makes a spiteful comment to Elizabeth about the removal of the soldiers to Brighton causing pain to her family. After the guests depart, Miss Bingley criticises Elizabeth to Darcy but he crushes her by announcing that he now considers Elizabeth 'one of the handsomest women of my acquaintance'.

Commentary: **Miss Bingley's attempt to embarrass Elizabeth backfires as she actually upsets Georgiana by her implied reference to Wickham, and this damages Miss Bingley further in Darcy's eyes.**

Elizabeth has acquired a suntan on her travels, which makes her seem a fresh creature of the great outdoors rather than a feeble inhabitant of the stifling parlours which are the milieu of the Bingley sisters. As we know from Chapter 7, Darcy admires women with colour in their cheeks and bright eyes.

Chapter 46

Elizabeth finds two letters from Jane: the first relates that Lydia has eloped with Wickham, the second that there is no word from the couple and that they may not be married yet, so their father has gone to London to find them. Elizabeth is devastated, realising that if Wickham does not marry her youngest sister, the reputations of both Lydia and the entire family will be ruined. As Elizabeth is about to rush out to find the Gardiners, Darcy appears and she explains to him the situation. She and Darcy blame themselves for not exposing Wickham. The Gardiners take Elizabeth home to Longbourn immediately.

Commentary: **Paradise has been spoiled by the deceitful and insinuating Wickham and the naive and reckless Lydia. In the following chapters letters are the essential means of three-way communication between Hertfordshire, Derbyshire and London. Here the seriousness of the situation is conveyed by the dramatic, flustered writing style of the normally calm Jane. Darcy can now play the role of hero and saviour to prove he deserves Elizabeth's love, and that he can take care of her family better than her father.**

Chapter 47

Mr Gardiner attempts to reassure his niece that Wickham will certainly marry Lydia because he will not want his own career and reputation

> **Context**
>
> A suntan was to be avoided by ladies — hence the use of parasols — as it was a characteristic of agricultural workers and therefore perceived as low-class.

> **Context**
>
> For an unmarried daughter to be alone in the company of a man who was not a relative was scandalous; the loss of her reputation would mean utter disgrace and social exclusion for both the girl and her family. Thus an elopement and hasty wedding ceremony, while not at all proper, were preferable. See extended discussion in 'Manners and morals', pp. 84–85, and 'Gretna Green', p. 87.

ruined. Elizabeth replies by telling them generally about Wickham's past behaviour, without revealing the details of his liaison with Darcy's sister. At Longbourn Mrs Bennet is hysterical, blaming Colonel Forster for not taking care of her daughter. In private, Jane assures Elizabeth that there was no way anyone could have known about their sister's attachment to Wickham. They examine the letter that Lydia left for Colonel Forster's wife, in which she looks forward to signing her name 'Lydia Wickham'.

Commentary: **A day and a half's journey home stretches out the horror and suspense before they can learn of Lydia's fate, and this is further deferred by no word having come from Mr Bennet in London. Mrs Bennet, typically, has taken to her bed, where she is indulging in wild fantasies, blaming everyone but herself, and worrying about Lydia's wedding clothes. Elizabeth and Jane feel guilty about having kept Wickham's nature a secret from the rest of the family.**

Chapter 48

Mr Gardiner follows Mr Bennet to London and writes a few days later with the news that the search for the couple has been unsuccessful. Mr Collins writes to accuse the Bennets of poor parenting and notes that Lydia's behaviour reflects badly on the family as a whole. Mr Gardiner writes to say that all attempts to trace Wickham have failed, and that Mr Bennet is returning home.

Commentary: **The urgent and futile quest for the missing couple in the metropolis is as near as Austen gets to mystery and drama. The self-congratulatory letter from Mr Collins is a monument to his hypocrisy and that of his profession — telling parents they would be better off if their child were dead is not a notably Christian sentiment — though his condemnation of the 'faulty degree of indulgence' granted to Lydia is valid. Austen frequently uses minor characters in this economical way, whereby even the most obtuse and reprehensible ones are able to draw the right conclusion, even though it reflects badly on them that they are heartless or tactless enough to do so. Wickham's reputation deteriorates even further with the information that not only has he left debts, but that he is a gambler.**

Mr Bennet's moment of recognition of his own failings is brief, and he characteristically turns to making fun of his wife and teasing Kitty.

Chapter 49

Mr Gardiner writes to tell Mr Bennet that Wickham and Lydia have been found and that Wickham will marry her if the Bennets will guarantee him a small income. Mr Bennet agrees, deciding that marriage to a scoundrel is better than a ruined reputation. The Bennets assume that the Gardiners have paid Wickham a sizable amount to get him to agree to the wedding, and that they owe a deep debt to their relatives. Mrs Bennet rises from her bed and is deliriously happy at having Lydia married, even under such circumstances.

Commentary: **Mr Gardiner proves himself a much more efficient manager than his brother-in-law, having found the runaways and arranged a marriage settlement. An astute reader will already realise who the provider of the ten thousand pounds must be. Austen makes it clear that neither of Lydia's parents has learned anything from her disastrous elopement, the result of their negligence, indolence and wrong priorities.**

> ...marriage to a scoundrel is better than a ruined reputation

Chapter 50

Mrs Bennet is peeved that her husband refuses to allow the couple to visit, or to provide Lydia with money to purchase clothes. Elizabeth's opinion of Darcy has changed so completely that if he were to propose to her again, she would accept him. She understands, however, that, given Lydia's shameful elopement and the addition of Wickham to the Bennet family, there is now a 'gulf impassable' between them. Mr Gardiner writes to inform Mr Bennet that Wickham has accepted a military commission in Newcastle, and after persuasion by Jane and Elizabeth, Mr Bennet allows the newlyweds to call in on their way north.

Commentary: **Mrs Bennet shows how morally bankrupt she is by caring more about Lydia's lack of fine clothing than that she has been living in sin. By contrast with Mr Collins and their father, Elizabeth and Jane are able to extend charity towards Lydia even though both have suffered through her misbehaviour.**

Chapter 51

Lydia and Wickham seem oblivious to all the trouble they have caused. Lydia describes her wedding and lets slip that Darcy was in the church. Elizabeth is amazed and sends a letter to Mrs Gardiner asking for an explanation.

Commentary: **Lydia is, as always, 'untamed, unabashed, wild, noisy, and fearless'. Her taking precedence, as a married woman, over Jane is shockingly insensitive, as is her blithe offer to find a husband for her and Elizabeth. She breaks her promise, a serious fault, by revealing Darcy's presence at the wedding, and does not recognise her debt of gratitude to the Gardiners.**

Chapter 52

Mrs Gardiner replies to Elizabeth that Darcy indeed found Lydia and Wickham and paid the money that facilitated the marriage, but that he does not wish this to become known. She drops hints that his love for Elizabeth is the reason for his actions. Elizabeth lets Wickham know that she has learned the truth about him.

Commentary: **Aunt Gardiner says that Darcy's real fault, now that he is no longer proud, is obstinacy — in which case he will never give up Elizabeth — and a lack of liveliness, which she will be able to provide.**

Chapter 53

TASK **8**

Chapter 53 offers a very striking example of a mirrored event — Darcy and Bingley arrive at Netherfield, but in circumstances very different from those of Chapter 1. Try to find other examples of paired or opposite events in the novel.

After Wickham and Lydia depart, news arrives that Bingley is returning to Netherfield for a few weeks. Mr Bennet refuses to visit him. Three days after his arrival, however, Bingley visits the Bennets, accompanied by Darcy. Mrs Bennet is overly attentive to Bingley and rude to Darcy, unaware that he saved Lydia. The gentlemen promise to dine at Longbourn soon.

Commentary: **The novel has come full circle and repeats the arrival of Bingley and Darcy in the neighbourhood, but the two men and two women concerned are now wiser than they were a year ago. Once again Elizabeth has a secret not shared with the rest of her family — that Darcy was their salvation — and this once again causes embarrassment.**

Chapter 54

Darcy and Bingley dine at Longbourn; Bingley sits next to Jane, but Darcy and Elizabeth are unable to converse.

Commentary: **The suspense as to whether Darcy will renew his address to Elizabeth is prolonged by their lack of any opportunity to speak in private. Thus were the frustrations of courtship among the gentry, whose every move was governed by etiquette.**

Chapter 55

Bingley visits the Bennets a few days later, and eagerly accepts a dinner invitation for the following day. After the meal, Mrs Bennet manages, clumsily, to leave Bingley alone with Jane, but he does not propose. The following day, however, Bingley goes shooting with Mr Bennet and stays for dinner. When he finds himself alone with Jane he finally proposes, and Jane tells Elizabeth that she is 'the happiest creature in the world'. She has learnt that Bingley had no idea that she was in London over the winter, because his sisters were determined to keep him away from her.

Commentary: **The only reason for the delay in Bingley proposing to Jane is to keep the Bennets and the reader in suspense (and temporarily to thwart Mrs Bennet's clumsy scheming). We know that if Bingley proposes to Jane, then it is likely that Darcy will propose to Elizabeth, so much have their fates become intertwined by this stage.**

Chapter 56

A week after Bingley and Jane become engaged, Lady Catherine de Bourgh appears unannounced at Longbourn, wanting to speak with Elizabeth. Lady Catherine informs Elizabeth that she has heard a rumour that she and Darcy are planning to marry. She insists the idea is ridiculous, given Elizabeth's low station in life and the tacit engagement of Darcy to her own daughter. Elizabeth admits that she and Darcy are not engaged but, despite his aunt's bullying, refuses to promise not to enter into an engagement to him in the future. Lady Catherine leaves, furious and frustrated.

Commentary: **Elizabeth, 'a gentleman's daughter', defeats her ladyship in a sparring match of language and logic, and delivers a blow against the aristocracy and their autocratic ways. Ironically, the two women are similar in being 'obstinate' and 'headstrong', but the elder has no charm or wit to make these qualities attractive. Though Lady Catherine's objections to the Bennet family are valid, the reader's sympathies must be firmly with Elizabeth.**

Chapter 57

A letter arrives from Mr Collins for Mr Bennet warning that Lady Catherine will not approve of an engagement between Darcy and Elizabeth. Mr Bennet is hugely entertained but Elizabeth cannot laugh with him.

Commentary: **Mr Bennet's enjoyment of the absurd and his prejudice against Mr Collins blinds him to the possibility of there being any truth in the engagement rumour. His philosophy 'For what do we live, but to make sport for our neighbours, and laugh at them in our turn?' is not supported by Austen, whose work suggests that she believed one should treat serious matters seriously.**

❮ Top ten *quotation*

TASK 9

Lady Catherine's unintended encouragement of Darcy is one of many instances in the text where the reader's attention is drawn to 'irony'. Austen is generally described as a great 'ironist'. What do you understand by this? What is the effect on the reader? Pick three other examples from the novel and think about the effect each of them has.

Context

Pemberley is the equivalent of a character in the novel, so important a role does it play. See the section 'The significance of locations' (pp. 75–77) for a discussion of the real and imagined locations used by Austen.

objective correlative

an object, situation or event that is used to signify characters or emotions

Chapter 58

Darcy returns from London to stay with Bingley at Netherfield. The two friends visit the Bennets, and everyone takes a walk together. Elizabeth and Darcy lag behind, and when they are alone, Elizabeth thanks him for his generosity in saving Lydia's good name. Darcy replies that he did so only because Lydia is her sister. He then says that his feelings toward her have not changed since his proposal. Elizabeth tells him that her own feelings have changed, and that she is now willing to marry him.

Commentary: **It is a fitting irony that Lady Catherine's interference has had the opposite of the desired effect in giving Darcy encouragement to propose again. The lovers admit they have both had to learn hard but necessary lessons about pride and prejudice, for which they are mutually grateful.**

Chapter 59

Elizabeth tells a stunned Jane that she has agreed to marry Darcy. The next evening Darcy asks Mr Bennet for his consent to the match. Mr Bennet needs Elizabeth to convince him that she does indeed care for Darcy, and she tells him how Darcy paid off Wickham. Mrs Bennet learns of her second daughter's engagement and is suitably ecstatic.

Commentary: **Elizabeth's teasing remark to Jane that she fell in love with Darcy when she saw 'his beautiful grounds at Pemberley' is not entirely humorous, which the reader can appreciate, though Jane cannot. At that point she recognised the real Darcy through the objective correlative of his surroundings and possessions. She saw the social security and distance from her embarrassing family that the place could offer, and felt the romantic attraction of becoming the princess of the fairy-tale palace.**

Mr Bennet feelingly reminds Elizabeth, and the reader, of the need for respect and esteem in a happy marriage. The nearest portrayal of this ideal in Austen's work, one which goes beyond the first few weeks after the wedding, is in fact the marriage of the Gardiners.

Chapter 60

Darcy and Elizabeth discuss how their love began and developed. Darcy informs Lady Catherine of his engagement, while Elizabeth communicates the situation to Mrs Gardiner. Mr Bennet writes to Mr Collins. The Collinses come to Lucas Lodge to escape an angry Lady Catherine.

Commentary: **Relatives have been almost universally the cause of difficulty and distress for the hero and heroine, and it is therefore not surprising that they are looking forward to being able to choose the company they keep in future.**

Chapter 61

After the weddings, Bingley purchases an estate near Pemberley and the Bennet sisters visit one another frequently. Kitty is kept away from Lydia and her bad influence, and she matures greatly by spending time with Jane and Elizabeth. Lydia and Wickham remain incorrigible, asking Darcy for money and sponging off the Bingleys. Elizabeth becomes great friends with Georgiana, and Lady Catherine eventually accepts the marriage and visits her nephew and his wife at Pemberley. Darcy and Elizabeth continue to consider the Gardiners close friends, grateful for the fact that they brought Elizabeth to Pemberley the first time and helped to bring the couple together.

Commentary: **Austen uses the authorial 'I' to tie up the ends in the final chapter. The last words in the novel are 'uniting them', union being the aim of comedy. By convention there are multiple weddings for the finale of a comedy, and the work has 'the happiest, wisest, most reasonable end'.**

The villains conveniently reform themselves enough to at least accept the outcome they fought so hard to avoid, and those with minds capable of being moulded receive the best of instruction hereafter.

*TASK **10***

Are you happy with the novel's ending? Sketch out or write an alternative conclusion which is consistent with the characters as we know them.

Themes

The title of the novel comes from a sentence in Fanny Burney's *Cecilia* (1782). Pride was the first and worst of the seven deadly sins. Pride is different to vanity: pride relates more to our opinion of ourselves, vanity to what we would have others think of us.

TASK 11

The faults of pride and prejudice are not limited to Darcy and Elizabeth. Before you read the paragraphs on Darcy's pride and Elizabeth's prejudice, which other characters do you consider display either or both of these vices?

Themes are the fundamental and often universal ideas explored in a literary work. The opening chapter sets up the expectation that the story will be about courtship and marriage; the financial and social considerations involved in the need to catch husbands for the girls are made clear from the outset.

The original title of the novel, *First Impressions*, conveys a warning not to judge, or pre-judge (the meaning of 'prejudice') from first and therefore inevitably superficial impressions. Austen does not subscribe to the concept of love at first sight. It was an important moral doctrine at the time that choice (a word with spiritual connotations) should be based on fact and not rushed into because of habit, the authority of someone else, a partial (in both senses) view, purely sensory perceptions or personal interest. First impressions are often unsound and delusory, suspiciously close to being products of the imagination rather than of reason, and should always be resisted by a right-thinking and prudent person.

Pride: Darcy and others

In addition to Darcy, other characters in the novel are guilty of pride (i.e. of having an excessively high opinion of themselves or behaving with conceit, arrogance or disdain). Elizabeth calls it 'discernment' but this is just a form of pride. She has a high opinion of her wit and ability to amuse through being critical, which her father is also guilty of and encourages in her. Mary Bennet suffers from an unjustified complacency about her own abilities and 'was always impatient for display' (p. 25), though, according to her own definition, this is more vanity than pride. The Bingley sisters and Lady Catherine are other contenders, and Mr Collins must be awarded a star prize, for although he appears obsequious, this does not detract from his real opinion of himself that he is supremely deserving and justifiably appreciated. He is in a 'state of angry pride' after being rejected by Elizabeth. Many characters discuss pride and vanity, thereby making it a recurring motif. Nearly everyone is accused of it at some stage, even timid Georgiana Darcy (by Wickham).

Reserve can often be interpreted as pride — and Darcy's sister is also shy — but Darcy is in fact too proud in not bothering to correct the impression he gives of being proud. Mrs Bennet declares him to be 'so high and so conceited' and 'ate up with pride'. Even Kitty calls him a 'tall, proud man', and although we cannot trust their judgements they are saying what everyone else is also thinking. His comment on Elizabeth is disdainful and he does not take care that she should not overhear him. The comment is itself a proud one: 'not handsome enough to tempt me' — as though he deserves better than anyone else. His being a man of few words implies he may not think others worth talking to.

He expects Elizabeth not only to accept his first lordly proposal but to be grateful for it. Marriage to one person meant 'connections' to many others and Darcy has too high an opinion of himself, having been spoilt from birth, to think it appropriate that either he, or anyone in his social circle, should become connected to the Bennet family. This belief causes pain to Jane and to Elizabeth on her behalf. Elizabeth describes his letter explaining his actions as 'all pride and insolence'; his interference in the affairs of his friend could have damaged Bingley's future happiness. In the end, however, Elizabeth tells her father that Darcy has no 'improper pride', even though he himself has owned up to the fault.

Prejudice: Elizabeth and others

In addition to Elizabeth, other characters in the novel are guilty of prejudice (i.e. a preconceived or irrational adverse judgement without examination of the facts of the particular case). Mrs Bennet has preconceived views on just about everything, and gossip and prejudice feed off each other. Mrs Gardiner is influenced by hearing that Darcy was 'formerly spoken of as a very proud, ill-natured boy', but changes her opinion later after receiving the testimony of one who knows, his housekeeper. The inhabitants of Meryton decide after only one evening that Darcy is 'the proudest, most disagreeable man in the world'. Lady Catherine constantly proclaims what is and what is not acceptable on every matter under the sun, including governesses and 'coming out'. Mr Collins's misconceptions about women count as a prejudice towards the other sex. People in trade were looked down upon by the aristocracy and landed gentry (the latter represented by the Bingley sisters) and Darcy has inherited this prejudice; later he learns from meeting the Gardiners that some of them are worthy of his respect. Though he is right to be prejudiced against Elizabeth's mother and her younger sisters, he initially lumps the two older sisters in with this blanket dismissal and has to learn to be more discriminating.

Elizabeth's prejudice against Darcy causes her to fall into the trap of being uncritical and credulous of Wickham. She says later of Darcy and Wickham respectively: 'One has got all the goodness, and the other all the appearance of it.' It is a sign of her increased maturity that she has learnt to recognise the difference. She is 'resolved against any sort of

conversation' with Darcy at the Netherfield ball, since she is 'determined to hate' him, and has previously promised never to dance with him. She admits to Jane that she 'meant to be uncommonly clever in taking so decided a dislike to him without any reason', (i.e. that she was governed by prejudice) and this is also the cause of her double standards in criticising Charlotte for marrying for money but thinking it acceptable that Wickham should do the same with Miss King. Elizabeth's defect is to betray her own principles and 'wilfully to misunderstand' and she often jumps to conclusions; Jane is on several occasions nearer the mark in her explanations about other characters' behaviour. Ironically it is Elizabeth who tells Darcy that he should not be blinded by prejudice and that it is incumbent upon him to be 'secure of judging properly at first' (p. 92).

anagnorisis

moment of recognition by a character of an important truth

Top ten *quotation* >

It is reading Darcy's letter that convinces her that she has been mistaken about him, although she at first tries to block out his appeal by adopting 'a strong prejudice against every thing he might say' (p. 198). She then has her moment of **anagnorisis** when she recognises that she has been 'blind, partial, prejudiced, absurd'.

She must do penance awhile before emerging a chastened and better person. One cannot judge others if one knows not oneself; this is the basis of tragedy. Elizabeth is reborn when she says: 'Till this moment I never knew myself.' At the end of the novel she tells Darcy 'how gradually all [my] former prejudices had been removed'. Because of her prejudice she very nearly loses the perfect man.

Further themes

Reason

A word used nearly 100 times in the novel in grammatical variants of 'reason' and 'rational', reason is the fundamental precept that defines what it is to be human and divides the characters of *Pride and Prejudice* into distinct categories: those that think and those that do not. On p. 202 Elizabeth has a revelation that her sin has been to drive reason away and that the rest of her mistakes have automatically followed. Elizabeth confesses in Chapter 40 that she took a dislike to Darcy 'without any reason', but she can tell Lady Catherine: 'I am not to be intimidated into anything so wholly unreasonable' (p. 337). Ironically this stance is interpreted by her interlocutor as proof of her not being 'reasonable' (p. 339), and their verbal duel seems as much about who is the more rational as about a possible liaison between their families, since Elizabeth thinks (sarcastically) that Lady Catherine's journey to break off the supposed engagement 'was a rational scheme, to be sure!'

PHILIP ALLAN LITERATURE GUIDE **FOR A-LEVEL**

Darcy has reasons for everything he does, whereas all the other characters (except Mr Gardiner) fail in this area by either not showing any reasoning or by faulty rationalising. Even Mrs Gardiner, a sound thinker in many ways, is irrational in her belief that Wickham must be a nice young man because he comes from Derbyshire (her former home) and she initially condemns Darcy from hearsay as having been 'a very proud, ill-natured boy' (p. 141).

Reason is what must prevail for a work to be defined as a comedy, as pointed out by Elizabeth's comment on the engagement of Jane and Bingley: 'the happiest, wisest, most reasonable end!' (p. 328). Reflecting back at the end of the novel, 'How earnestly did she then wish that her former opinions had been more reasonable' (p. 355), she teases Darcy with the idea that it was 'perfectly reasonable' of him to fall in love with her because she was different from other women and he was 'sick of civility, of deference, of officious attention' (p. 359). On the next page the dialogue continues to talk about what is 'reasonable'.

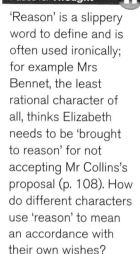

*Pause for **Thought***

'Reason' is a slippery word to define and is often used ironically; for example Mrs Bennet, the least rational character of all, thinks Elizabeth needs to be 'brought to reason' for not accepting Mr Collins's proposal (p. 108). How do different characters use 'reason' to mean an accordance with their own wishes?

Judgement

This is a moral imperative of biblical proportions, and the one that underpins the novel; pride and prejudice are lapses of judgement; until they know and can judge themselves, which is the journey Elizabeth and Darcy have to make, they make erroneous judgements of each other.

The reader in turn must exercise judgement on the characters and, to make this more challenging, the narrative viewpoint is often not to be trusted, so that we can make the same mistakes as Elizabeth does. The lively characters of Lydia and Wickham are the dangerous ones we should not be taken in by, but which we might be tempted to find attractive, especially in comparison to those who are staid or insipid.

The recognition of pretence and illusion is part of having judgement; if there is deception then the truth is being hidden, and it is a Christian duty to uncover truth and act upon it.

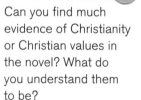

*Pause for **Thought***

Can you find much evidence of Christianity or Christian values in the novel? What do you understand them to be?

Upbringing

The Bennet sisters are quasi-orphans, having a pair of inadequate and neglectful parents, and are therefore at risk of falling into error and of becoming social victims. Lydia 'has never been taught to think on serious subjects' and 'has been allowed [...] to adopt any opinions that came in her way' (p. 269). The outcome of one's upbringing was believed to be a mixture of natural disposition and guidance, the latter considered more influential than formal education. Poor family role models are to blame for most errant behaviour in Austen. Mr Collins

was brought up by 'an illiterate and miserly father' (p. 69); Darcy was more fortunate in having been 'taught what was *right*' and 'given good principles' as a child, but his failings stem from not being taught to correct his temper, being spoilt for many years as an only child, and allowed to develop 'pride and conceit' (p. 349) until cured by Elizabeth.

Top ten *quotation* ❯

Moderation

Aristotle's precept of moderation in all things is the definition of decorum. Austen supported the Augustan tenet of restraint and was deeply wary of the forms of excess and self-indulgence that later characterised the Romantic movement. In particular she believed that moderation in speech and feeling was required for polite society to function without vulgarity and embarrassment. Deficiency is also a failure of moderation and is criticised in the guise of Mr and Mrs Bennet and, though more gently, in Jane and Bingley; being too pliant and amiable shows a want of discernment and independence. Lydia and her mother know no moderation of feeling or expression, nor do they exercise moderation in the pursuit of their goals; Mrs Bennet is either downcast to the point of taking to her bed or uncontainedly delighted. Mr Collins also represents excess in the novel; he talks for too long and overwhelms people, such as Mrs Philips who is 'awed by such an excess of good breeding' (p. 72), a contradiction in terms.

Balance

The marriage of Elizabeth and Darcy is a reconciling of energy and reason, the rambling and playful versus the rigid and regulated; significantly, 'uniting them' are the last two words of the novel. Balance is needed in human temperament too: Mr Collins originally had 'great humility of manner' but has gone to the other extreme of being conceited, and is now a contradictory 'mixture of pride and obsequiousness'. Comedy is predicated upon the concept of harmony by means of the eradication of extremes.

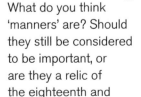

Pause for **Thought**

What do you think 'manners' are? Should they still be considered to be important, or are they a relic of the eighteenth and nineteenth centuries?

Manners

Although good manners are the hallmark of civility, unlike morals they can be counterfeited. Sir William Lucas and Wickham have notably courteous manners but these hide their moral weaknesses (vanity and fecklessness respectively) and an abdication of responsibility towards their professions and acquaintances, the latter more seriously than the former because his speech and actions are more deliberate. Those who talk only of their own interests are, by definition, bad-mannered.

Mr Collins likes to think he has good manners, but they are only an overdone affectation. In fact he pays no regard to his interlocutors and causes them frustration and embarrassment — with the exception of Lady Catherine, who accepts his fawning as nothing less than her due.

Gratitude

This is another biblical and romance theme. As humans should be grateful to their divine creator and benefactor, Wickham owes gratitude to Darcy for the support he received from the latter's father. Conversely, it is shocking to Elizabeth that Darcy has allegedly shown ingratitude to the son of the man his father admitted 'the greatest obligations' to. However, Collins's gratitude towards Lady Catherine is excessive and invites mockery of them both for the falsity of the relationship.

Gratitude was automatically owed to parents, and Jane and Elizabeth carry out their filial obligations, though with difficulty in the latter's case but the more to her credit because of that. Mr Gardiner is an important focus for gratitude for his having 'readily promised every assistance in his power' to support his sister's family, and it is telling that Mr Bennet, Elizabeth and Jane understand their obligation to their uncle, but that Mrs Bennet is insufficiently appreciative.

A bond of gratitude between the leading couple is mutual: Elizabeth's gratitude to Darcy for his efforts on Lydia's behalf, as well as her 'Gratitude, not merely for having once loved her, but for loving her still' (p. 253); his to her for having been 'taught a lesson [...] most advantageous', 'What do I not owe you!' (p. 349).

Improvement

Austen's heroines are required to select and finally acknowledge a beloved with whom they can undergo a process of mutual improvement. A suitable marriage is one of intelligent love where the partners can educate each other by offering the other what they are lacking in order to become Platonically complete: '...by her ease and liveliness, his mind might have been softened, his manners improved; and from his judgment, information, and knowledge of the world, she must have received benefit of greater importance' (p. 295). One is improved through lessons and reflecting on and learning from them. Darcy tells Elizabeth: 'You taught me a lesson... By you, I was properly humbled' (p. 349). His letter teaches Elizabeth a lesson about the dangers of prejudice by revealing how she was fooled by Wickham.

TASK 12

Elizabeth and Darcy are not the only characters who undergo 'improvement'. Find evidence that Kitty and Georgiana are also 'improved' at the end of the novel.

Characters

For a character map showing the relationships between the characters in *Pride and Prejudice*, see the Downloads for the book on the free website at **www.philipallan.co.uk/literatureguidesonline**.

Individual characters

Elizabeth Bennet

Elizabeth's fine dark eyes render her 'uncommonly intelligent' and she has a slight figure. Her family calls her 'Lizzy', her friends and neighbours call her 'Eliza', and the narrator calls her 'Elizabeth'. Frank, assertive, sensitive and spirited, she is the only sister who has 'quickness' of mind, which is appreciated by her father but a cause of puzzlement to her mother, to whom she is 'the least dear…of all her children'.

Elizabeth is the lens through which the action and the other characters of the novel are seen, and it is a lens with a flaw: a desire to be thought witty, a 'lively playful disposition, which delighted in anything ridiculous', and a 'lively imagination [which] soon settled it all' are attractive traits but also liabilities, and ones that lead to faulty judgement. It is 'her temper to be happy' (p. 231), however, so she is a true comedy heroine.

Elizabeth is far from perfect, and makes enemies because some perceive her behaviour to show 'conceit and impertinence', and because of her sarcasm (she tells Lady Catherine that being slighted and despised by the latter would be 'heavy misfortunes' p. 336). She is secretive on several occasions, even towards Jane and her father. She is too sure of her own judgements; she tells Jane, who is more right than she is about Darcy, that 'one knows exactly what to think'. She can be critical, intolerant and harsh in her judgements. Her outburst when she learns of Wickham's transference of attentions is sarcastic and extreme — 'I am sick of them all' — and her aunt reprimands her to 'Take care, Lizzy'. She finally learns clear-sightedness through her errors, which arise not only from false assumptions (i.e. prejudice) but also from pride because she is piqued by Darcy's rudeness about her at the assembly room ball. She was born to 'discover the falsehood of her own opinions, and to counteract, by her conduct, her most favourite maxims'.

Fitzwilliam Darcy

The hero possesses a fine French aristocratic name (originally d'Arcy), noble lineage, and a 'very satirical eye' which Elizabeth finds intimidating. He also has £10,000 a year, making him very rich. He is 'ashamed of his aunt's ill breeding', which is to his credit, as is his lack of interest in marrying his cousin Anne or his friend's sister, Caroline Bingley, simply for dynastic reasons. Family loyalty is strong, however, where his sister and ward, Georgiana, is concerned; he is described as 'the best of brothers'. Even Wickham allows that Darcy is 'a kind and careful guardian of his sister' and is 'liberal-minded, just, sincere, rational, honourable, and perhaps agreeable' — all the attributes which Austen approves of. However, Darcy persuades Bingley that Jane Bennet is not to be viewed as a serious marriage prospect, genuinely believing that she is indifferent to him, and this is the main obstacle to his winning Elizabeth. Ill at ease with strangers, pride is his failing and the cause of his prejudice against the Bennet family. Darcy also prides himself on his inflexibility: 'My good opinion once lost is lost for ever.' He is considered intellectual by the Bingleys for being a reader and using 'words of four syllables'.

Some readers are uncomfortable about the apparent sudden change in Darcy's character between the two halves of the novel. It could be said that the friendship of Darcy and Bingley never rings quite true, as they are so incompatible in interests and personality, and that Darcy's initial rudeness towards Elizabeth and damage to Jane's feelings can never be made up for in the reader's eyes. However, he has already started to appreciate Elizabeth before he leaves Netherfield, so the change in him is gradual rather than sudden, and he is still far from talkative, sociable or teasable even by the end. In any case Elizabeth changes too, and the point of their relationship is that they both have the power to change each other for the better, which is Austen's definition of a perfect couple.

There is never any suggestion that Darcy's morals are at fault, and we are told that he has always been popular on home ground. Jane constantly stands up for him, which prepares us for the discovery of his goodness, and the testimony of the Pemberley housekeeper gives a consistent overview of his character since a child. He makes one big mistake, which is to warn Bingley against Jane, but learns from this and apologises for having misjudged the situation. It is because he is at home, and not among strangers, when he meets Elizabeth at Pemberley that he can be his true self.

Darcy and Elizabeth have the power to change each other for the better

Mr Bennet

The head of the family is irresponsible as a father and husband. That Longbourn will be lost to the family on his death, though not his fault,

reflects badly on him as he has made no other provision for his wife and daughters. Although his ready wit makes him an appealing character, and he redeems himself somewhat at the end by at least recognising his negligence and accepting the blame for Lydia's elopement, he says immediately afterwards that it will not make a lasting impression.

He regards his children and his acquaintance as an author would his fictional creations: commenting on and criticising them drolly but without apparent personal feeling or involvement in their lives and fates. His creator summarises him as a 'mixture of quick parts, sarcastic humour, reserve and caprice'. This is not an admirable set of qualities, but he shares them with his favourite daughter, Elizabeth. He enjoys thwarting and baiting his wife and witnessing her disappointments, is amused by his daughters being 'crossed in love' and values his son-in-law Wickham because of his 'impudence and hypocrisy'.

He fails in his paternal responsibility to 'restrain the wild giddiness of his youngest daughters', preferring to laugh at them rather than 'exert himself', and Elizabeth has no illusions about 'the impropriety of her father's behaviour as a husband' (p. 228) or the moral inadequacy of his 'philosophic composure'. He represents the deadly sin of sloth because of his natural 'indolence'.

Mrs Bennet

Mrs Bennet fancies that she suffers from her 'nerves', is 'invariably silly', completely humourless and solely concerned with gossip and competing with her neighbours. She is also a tedious hypochondriac, which allows her husband to win sympathy for being long-suffering.

Mrs Bennet's vulgarity and gossiping are important elements of the plot as well as providing humour in the novel

Topham Picturepoint

PHILIP ALLAN LITERATURE GUIDE **FOR A-LEVEL**

Her vulgarity and materialism are a handicap to Jane and Elizabeth's prospects. Thanks to her talking loudly and boastfully of the expected union between Jane and Bingley, Darcy is alerted to the danger to his friend and the need to remove him from the vicinity. Her failure to set a good example to her five daughters almost leads to Lydia's 'irremediable infamy' and utter social disgrace.

Her creator describes Mrs Bennet as 'a woman of mean understanding, little information, and uncertain temper', and as having 'weak understanding and illiberal mind' (p. 7), which is damning criticism indeed. Her moods are 'violent', veering between the extremes of 'exuberance' and 'alarm'. Her illogicalities and inconsistencies are the main source of comedy in the novel. One might have some sympathy for a woman with five daughters to marry off, but we are not allowed to empathise with her because, as an unsatisfactory wife and mother 'incapable of exertion', she is one of the novel's major moral concerns.

Jane Bennet

Jane Bennet is often referred to as 'Miss Bennet', being the eldest daughter. She is considered, even by Darcy, as the prettiest of the sisters. She is trusting, unsceptical and passive to a degree some might call insipid, accepting without demur her abandonment by Bingley. Elizabeth tells her 'You never see a fault in anybody', which is more a failure of discernment than a gift of tolerance, since it entails being 'blind to the follies and nonsense of others' (p. 16). Though her 'mild and steady candour' is admirable, she does admit 'I know not what to think'. She refuses to believe that Caroline Bingley is capable 'of wilfully deceiving anyone' and insists on seeing everything and everyone 'in the best light', even after Lydia's disappearance. However, she is sometimes nearer the mark than Elizabeth, since she is free of both pride and prejudice; her being 'afraid of judging harshly' is a corrective to her sister's tendency to be overly critical.

Mary Bennet

The only plain one in the family, Mary spouts pompous platitudes. She has 'neither genius nor taste' and her bookishness does not impress anyone, any more than her bad piano playing and singing, though she does not have enough self-knowledge to recognise this. As a female equivalent of Mr Collins, she speaks in risible platitudes and mixed metaphors: 'we must stem the tide of malice, and pour into the wounded bosoms of each other, the balm of sisterly consolation' (p. 274). That 'Mary wished to say something very sensible, but knew not how' (p. 9) shows the reader that her creator did not approve of learning in isolation without access to experience.

❮ Top ten *quotation*

*Pause for **Thought***

Do you find Mrs Bennet a developed character or a stereotype? Some feminist critics feel she has often been judged too harshly, and point out that given Mr Bennet's apparent neglect, at least their daughters have *one* parent who takes an interest in securing their futures. Can you find any redeeming features in Austen's presentation of her?

Lydia Bennet

Lydia is described in the most derogatory terms: 'impertinent' and 'imprudent', 'self-willed and careless', guilty of 'wild volatility', 'wickedness', and 'ignorance and emptiness of mind'. She is incorrigible and irrational; she gives as her reason for buying an ugly hat that 'there were two or three much uglier in the shop'. She is loud, rude, indiscreet and morally irresponsible in eloping with Wickham and not caring whether it brings disgrace on her family. She is her mother's favourite, being most like her in character, and has inherited from her the traits of being 'a most determined talker', 'always unguarded and often uncivil'.

Careless about money as about everything else, she is also 'extremely fond of lottery tickets' and 'too eager in making bets', which is symbolic of her future gamble with her marriage and her life. Her body language is equally unrestrained and indecorous, as is shown by her giving a 'violent yawn' at the Netherfield ball. She is shameless to the end, when she begs for financial support from the husbands of her sisters.

Kitty (Catherine) Bennet

Two years older than Lydia, Kitty follows her younger sister in being a chaser of men and looks likely to end up the same way. Their father calls them 'two of the silliest girls in the country' (p. 30); they can talk of 'nothing but officers' who are 'dazzling with scarlet', and they are collectively 'ignorant, idle, and vain' and 'uncontrouled'.

Kitty's function is to be Lydia's partner and confidante, and to be a victim of her dominant personality to show the effect of bad influence. She is described as 'weak-spirited, irritable, and completely under Lydia's guidance', and 'affronted' by advice from her elder sisters.

George Wickham

Son of the former steward to old Mr Darcy, Wickham is a Cambridge graduate, a lieutenant in a county regiment and a gold-digger; there is obviously the suggestion of 'wicked' about his name. George, however, is a solidly reliable English name and the combination suggests his duplicity and his ability to fool even the most perceptive.

His 'most gentlemanlike appearance' is deceptive, since beneath the showy blue and red coats he is nothing but 'idle and frivolous gallantry' and he is described as 'very wild' (p. 237). Darcy accuses Wickham of 'vicious propensities' and of having led 'a life of idleness and dissipation'. He is 'profligate', 'false and deceitful', and 'insinuating' (p. 270), 'imprudent and extravagant' (p. 276). Money is his priority; Mary King's £10,000 a year attracts him away from Elizabeth. Later we learn from Darcy's housekeeper

Pause for **Thought**

Why do you think Austen created the Bennet family with five sisters? What would have been lost had there been fewer? Which one would you dispense with?

that he left debts behind him in Derbyshire, and the same is true of his sojourn in Meryton. Furthermore, he is a 'gamester' with gambling debts owed in Brighton of 'more than a thousand pounds'.

The Reverend William Collins

Rector of Hunsford in Kent, he is cousin and heir (as the only male relative) to Mr Bennet. He is 'not a sensible man'; his 'stupidity' is demonstrated by, amongst other things, his dislike of novels and his inability to win a single point at whist. He makes himself 'absurd' by his constant fawning on his noble patroness and his mannered language, particularly his studied compliments and clichés. Incapable of real feeling, he transfers his attentions from Jane to Elizabeth and from Elizabeth to Charlotte in a ridiculously short time when choosing the companion of his future life, as ordered by his Lady Catherine.

He is satirised throughout the novel for being 'irksome' and does nothing for the image of the clergy; he is 'a mixture of servility and self-importance' who, rather dubiously for a man of the cloth, plays cards for money, though very badly. He is presumptuous, introducing himself with 'impertinent freedom' to Darcy and invading Mr Bennet's study. His letter to Mr Bennet after Lydia's elopement is deeply offensive, crowned by his opinion that it would be better if Lydia were dead and his rejoicing that he didn't marry Elizabeth. He constantly reveals his own hypocrisy and unsuitability to be a member of the church.

❬ Top ten *quotation*

Charlotte Lucas

Charlotte is the eldest daughter of the Bennets' neighbours and rivals in Longbourn, and Elizabeth's closest friend. At the relatively advanced age of 27 she has a 'desire of an establishment' and knows that she cannot afford to turn down any offers of one. She settles down to a life of being bored by her husband and patronised by Lady Catherine in the vicarage in the village of Hunsford, keeping herself busy with her poultry. She represents the expectations for women at the time, expectations that Elizabeth refuses to accept. She understands Elizabeth better than she understands herself, knowing that 'her friend's dislike [of Darcy] would vanish, if she could suppose him to be in her power' thereby proving the extent to which Elizabeth is prejudiced.

Sir William Lucas

After his presentation at court and award of a knighthood Sir William was quick to give up his business and residence and move to Meryton, where he could lord it over the locals. He has given himself the airs of gentility but they are only skin deep as he is an uncaring parent and tactless host whose only aim is to name-drop and show off. His function

in the novel is to show that manners ('civilities') without morals are valueless, and that the more effusive the style the more superficial and suspect the content.

Lady Catherine de Bourgh

Widow of Sir Lewis de Bourgh, of Rosings Park in Kent, Lady Catherine, as well as being a comic caricature (and model for Oscar Wilde's Lady Bracknell), is a plot device to prevent the union of Darcy and Elizabeth. She is opinionated, selfish and pretentious, qualities which Austen constantly mocks, and these characteristics are reflected in her unaccommodating Norman castle of a name.

Darcy is her nephew through her deceased sister, Anne Fitzwilliam Darcy. Lady Catherine's daughter, also Anne, has a 'sickly constitution' and lacks accomplishments, but she is the Rosings heir and, according to her mother, Darcy's intended bride to unite the two estates and keep everything in the family. Anne is a cipher in the novel, and cannot exert herself to speak, thus giving the impression that she has been crushed by her domineering mother.

Lady Catherine constantly interferes in the domestic arrangements of Hunsford and gives unsolicited advice to everyone she meets. Elizabeth describes her as 'arrogant' and 'conceited'; Wickham confirms that she is 'dictatorial and insolent'; Darcy is 'ashamed of his aunt's ill-breeding' while Mr Collins attempts to recommend her as being 'all affability and condescension'.

Colonel Fitzwilliam

As another army officer, Darcy's pleasant cousin provides a foil against which Wickham can be judged. His manners are 'much admired' and therefore he is also a contrast to his cousin, with whom he is co-guardian of Georgiana. He would like to propose to Elizabeth but cannot afford to. He sets a good example in valuing someone for their own qualities and not their relatives; he also shows the constraints imposed on choice of partner by lack of income and the injustices inherent in being a younger son.

Georgiana Darcy

Darcy's sister is 'exceedingly shy' and not an appropriate match for Bingley. Her role is to be a victim of Wickham and an explanation of Darcy's hatred for him. When Darcy tells Elizabeth he wishes to present his sister to her, we know that he must still have hopes of an alliance with her. Elizabeth recognises in Georgiana family traits that cast light on her brother's reserve and support his claim that he does not know what to say to strangers.

Pause for **Thought**

Lady Catherine is the only true aristocrat in the novel. Can you infer anything about Austen's attitude to the nobility from her portrayal of Lady Catherine?

46

Charles Bingley

While the neighbourhood declares him to be 'amiable', Elizabeth tellingly accuses Bingley of a 'want of proper resolution'. His weakness shows in his allowing Darcy to persuade him that Jane is not interested in him and to drop his acquaintance with her despite being attracted. He says proudly of himself (p. 42) that 'Whatever I do is done in a hurry', exposing his lack of sense and reason.

Darcy admits that Bingley has 'stronger dependence on my judgement than on his own', which is a serious lack of moral fibre and could have led to tragic consequences in a different genre of novel. He is not clever, unlike his friend, but is 'sensible, good humoured, lively' (p. 16) and makes a suitable partner for Jane.

Caroline Bingley

The younger of Charles's sisters, she fancies herself as Darcy's future wife. She mocks Elizabeth and criticises her family to make Elizabeth seem common in Darcy's eyes. Worth £20,000 a year, she looks down on the inhabitants and entertainments of Meryton, comparing country life unfavourably to town life and being generally superior. Her jealousy of Elizabeth ironically makes Darcy more, not less, interested in her rival by drawing his attention to Elizabeth with her vicious comments.

Louisa (Bingley) Hurst

Like Caroline, Louisa is 'proud and conceited' and guilty of 'superciliousness'. The sisters are only distinguished from each other by the elder sister saying and doing less, presumably since she does not need to compete to attract a husband. Since it is unthinkable that Jane and Elizabeth could ever argue, it is interesting that Louisa and Caroline are in 'danger of hating each other' if they have to spend time alone together.

Mr Hurst

Always seen eating, idling or sleeping, Mr Hurst provides a foil for Bingley, who is more lively, amiable and considerate than his brother-in-law, and for Darcy, who is much more abstemious, and a reader rather than a card player. His apparently loveless relationship with Mrs Hurst is an example of a bad marriage and a lesson in what should be avoided.

Mr and Mrs Gardiner

Edward Gardiner is Mrs Bennet's brother, a 'sensible, gentlemanlike man' who is 'well bred and agreeable', but his occupation in trade is considered insufficiently genteel by the Bingley sisters and Lady Catherine, and even Darcy agrees that it must lessen the chances of the Bennet sisters marrying

well. The Gardiners have four young children, 'two girls of six and eight years old and two younger boys'. This is apparently so that the Gardiners' commitment to sorting out the mess in the Bennet family can be seen as all the more selfless when they have their own large family to support on their limited finances. The function of the Gardiners is a moral one, to show that one should judge by behaviour and not by wealth or its source. Mrs Gardiner is the voice of objective perception and reason in the novel, and gives Elizabeth good advice on several occasions, whilst also knowing when to keep silent. Elizabeth values Mr Gardiner's 'intelligence, his taste, [...] his good manners'. They are better parents in every way than the Bennets, and in addition they have the important qualities of 'cheerfulness', 'affection and intelligence'.

Mr and Mrs Philips

Mr Philips is the attorney at Meryton, married to Mrs Bennet's sister. Their presence in Meryton is an excuse for Lydia to go there to see the soldiers. Mrs Philips visits Longbourn to gossip with her sister. Her husband is described derogatorily as 'the broad-faced stuffy uncle Philips, breathing port wine'. Their role is to provide evidence for the reservations various characters have about belonging to or marrying into the Bennet family.

Character types

In this novel, characterisation is conveyed through narrative and dialogue rather than through description. The characters' credibility and individuality is achieved largely through their own speech, whereby they are presented as personae in a drama who independently reveal themselves through their utterances and how they relate to what the other characters have said just before, and which often gives a different impression from the one intended or assumed to have been conveyed.

Austen has been criticised for including only a narrow range of social types in her works. The world of Austen characters consists mainly of families or couples living in rural surroundings, who receive occasional visits from relatives. The age range is also restricted, since the elderly and children below the middle teens rarely appear as named characters. The middle-level rural gentry are the staple of her novels, not only because this is the world she knew, but because by creating a contained and homogeneous social sample every gradation of speech and behaviour within it becomes significant and comparisons are inescapable. Deviance from conformity to acceptable standards cannot be explained by differences of background if they have all shared it, and can therefore be attributed to lack of morals and/or deficiencies of upbringing.

Simple and complex characters

Jane and Bingley are simple, and so is their love. They are both incapable of taking the initiative, of being unamiable or of asserting their own views. Jane occasionally says something valid but only as an expression of her unswerving commitment to being kind, not because she is exercising any discriminatory judgement. Lydia is simple in being so single-minded; she cannot be made to exercise restraint or show shame when she has failed to do so. Charlotte Lucas is essentially simple, since she reacts logically and predictably to her situation in life both before and after becoming Mrs Collins, and it is this very straightforwardness and placidity that Elizabeth finds frustrating. Charlotte's father's function is to provide an example of and warning against snobbery and sycophancy, and to be the cause of embarrassment in his insensitive attempt to persuade Darcy and Elizabeth to dance together.

Lady Catherine and Mr Collins are comic caricatures representing pride. Mrs Bennet is the same character at the end of the novel as she is at its beginning, having learned nothing from the experiences her family has been through. The Caroline Bingley the reader sees never falters in her unpleasantness to the Bennets and pursuit of Darcy, thus making her a 'flat' character, though at least she has a distinctive persona, unlike her cipher of a sister. Mr Gardiner rises to the occasion in the saving of Lydia, but in a way entirely consistent with the reader's expectations.

It could be argued that the function of the simple characters is to cause things to happen to the complex characters, who would never have got themselves into such a situation without them. Simple characters also provide a foil for the complex characters who shine by contrast, since they are capable of thinking and feeling on an entirely different plane, whether good or evil. An intricate character is aware of implications and capable of judgement and choice, even if they make the wrong one.

Wickham is not simple because he presents a different face to different people, is fully aware of how he appears to others, and of the impropriety of his behaviour, but chooses to continue to misbehave for personal gain, relying on his ability to charm, persuade and ingratiate himself. He deliberately manipulates both Darcy and Elizabeth and is therefore guilty of active malice rather than the passive sin of ignorance. Mr Bennet has moments of self-realisation and self-judgement that show there is more to him than just a comic stereotype. It is when the two types clash, as in the proposal of Collins to Elizabeth, when both the moral dimension and the humour of the novel become most acute.

…the function of the simple characters is to cause things to happen to the complex characters

Pairs of characters and siblings

It was a convention of romance and eighteenth-century literature to create pairs of characters who were either indistinguishably similar or complete opposites. Bingley reveals the greater intelligence and complexity of Darcy's mind, just as Jane does for Elizabeth's mind. They are both foils for the main characters, and also a similar pair in being too undiscerning and amiable. Their existence allows for a double wedding to be planned within one family, a convention of comedy.

Obviously Darcy and Wickham are presented as a hero/villain pairing, which is reversed in the course of the narrative. The Bennet parents are opposites in character but similar, though for different reasons, in their neglect of their daughters, thus drawing attention to the dangers of both excess and deficiency. Charlotte and Elizabeth form an opposite pair, to be compared in their manner of responding to proposals. Mr Collins and Lady Catherine are the two comic villains who compete in odiousness and pomposity.

Mrs Hurst and Miss Bingley are presented as a pair of ugly sisters to Elizabeth's Cinderella. Kitty has the potential to develop into another Lydia, saved at the last by their separation.

Form, structure and language

Form

Comedy

Austen was influenced by eighteenth-century writers such as Jonathan Swift and Samuel Johnson and allies herself with their conservative and rational world view by using social comedy as her main mode. They embraced a nostalgia for and emulation of the classics — that is the literary practices and social values of Greek and Roman antiquity. These include a belief that only the intellect can raise us above an existence otherwise indistinguishable from that of animals, which live by their instincts and appetites. Elegance of expression and control of form are civilised virtues, and universal concerns are more enduring and important than those pertaining to the individual. As Dr Johnson said in *Rasselas* (1759), it is the job of a writer to examine the species not the individual, 'to remark general properties and large appearance' rather than to 'number the streaks of the tulip'. The aim of classical writing is therefore usually **didactic** (vice and virtue are debated and characters are punished or rewarded), hence the tendency towards satire and parody. Other features of style that Austen borrowed from the essayists are restraint and balance. Classical texts are usually urban and social, and dialogue, debate and rhetoric are the dominant modes and devices.

didactic with the intention of teaching the reader and instilling moral values

Social comedy

Eighteenth-century literature favoured social comedy as a genre as people of that period enjoyed satirising institutions and stereotypes. The drama of the period had developed from the comedies of humours by Ben Jonson and other early seventeenth-century dramatists, in which a character who embodies a 'humour' (e.g. melancholy) causes amusement when interacting with other character types. The Restoration plays at the end of the seventeenth century picked up these characteristics when the theatres re-opened, and exaggeration and scurrilous wit continued to

be the main feature of the eighteenth-century stage. One feels that the comic plays of Sheridan were never far from Austen's mind when she was creating dialogue for her silly and pretentious characters.

Austen wrote comic novels in the sense that the good are rewarded and the bad are punished, though not seriously, and no one dies. The plots end in marriage; in the case of *Pride and Prejudice* the conventional Shakespearean comedy ending of triple nuptials is employed. Austen's novels fall specifically into the genre of social comedy, sometimes called 'comedy of manners' (dealing with public behaviour and relationships); it is in relation to speech and actions towards others that the characters judge each other and the reader judges them.

The classical literary tradition (as opposed to the Romantic one, which deals with solitude and introspection: see p. 54 of this guide) is based on Plato's philosophy that individual people are only complete when they have found their complementary other half and soul mate and are members of society; this enables them to compare themselves to others and learn from them how to perfect themselves.

Comedy of manners

Austen's social comedy mocks the attitudes and behaviour of particular social groups, usually those that consider themselves fashionable and superior. Comedies of manners are necessarily set in interiors; drawing rooms where people meet, mix and reveal themselves. It is a didactic genre as well as an entertaining one, dependent on intelligence, wit and nuance of language.

Money and property are of paramount importance in social comedy, and expediency a driving force; to put it at its lowest, the world depicted by Austen is a market place dedicated to 'selling teenage virginity for cash and crenellations' (A. A. Gill, *Sunday Times Culture*, 6 January 2008). Austen's works conform to Horace Walpole's dictum: 'This world is a comedy to those that think, a tragedy to those that feel.' She encourages thinking rather than feeling, and therefore, like Chaucer, another observer of social mores, she is able to perceive the ludicrous and therefore identify the targets for satire, often those who claim to have feeling (like Mrs Bennet who suffers from her 'poor nerves' and has to retire to bed when anything upsetting happens) and who do no thinking at all.

For Austen, sense was more important than sensibility, and certainly necessary for a healthy individual life and a robust social system, in which sound choices are based on knowledge and judgement. Her aim is to make it possible for someone perceptive and sensitive to be able to reconcile themselves to their relationships and place in the social context, flawed though this is. Feelings of a deep and private nature are not expressed by the characters of her novels; even when struck by embarrassment and remorse her heroines are most concerned about justice, propriety, decorum and other social virtues. They consider how they will be perceived by others, rather than how they will survive their personal anguish. We are told as a matter of fact that Elizabeth thinks she has lost Darcy and Pemberley, but as readers we do not experience her suffering. How different from the next generation of female writers, such as the Brontës, who revealed their own emotions in their writing and allowed their heroines — think of Cathy in *Wuthering Heights* — to do the same.

> Feelings of a deep and private nature are not expressed by the characters

Romance

The romance genre pertains to adventure, heroic exploits, the winning of love and the facing of obstacles. Literature has utilised this formula since the medieval period, and still does; the idea of the course of true love not running smooth provided the basis for Arthurian legends, Shakespeare's comedy and much modern fiction in book and film form. It can be turned to both comedy and tragedy, depending on whether the lovers are separated (by death or imprisonment) or united at the end. The prerequisite for either is that the lovers should be idealised or exceptional, that the misunderstandings should be serious, that the opposition should be threatening, that chance, irony and fate should play significant parts, and that the future happiness or misery of the couple should be indisputable. These criteria can all be successfully applied to *Pride and Prejudice*. The novel approaches the tragic when Elizabeth realises what she has thrown away and thinks it is too late to alter the situation; comedy then appears in the unlikely form of Lady Catherine who, by attempting to ensure a tragic outcome, in fact brings about a comic resolution typical in its multiple marriages and trouncing or humbling of enemies. Darcy's performance as combatant against his evil enemy, Wickham, and as saviour of Lydia in order to please Elizabeth, makes him a quintessential romantic hero.

Romantic comedy novels traditionally stop just before or just after the wedding ceremony, and often with the fairy-tale ending of a betrothal and the promise of happy ever after. We do not know what transpires later in the relationship and do not witness its possible transformation to mundanity and disillusionment. We can see, however, that something went badly wrong with the Bennets' marriage, and their function in the novel is as a warning to Elizabeth and to the reader of the importance of judging by temperament and intelligence rather than, or at least as well as, physical attraction when choosing a partner for life.

Romance character types

The traditional characteristics of romance (and biblical) stories are: love between the rich and powerful (usually male) and the poor and humble (usually female), quests and rescues, heroes and villains, dragons and fairies, extremes of temperament between siblings, absent or invalid mothers and distant or tyrannical fathers, headstrong and unheeding sons or daughters. These features became transmuted and more subtle over time, but they are still discernible in Austen's character types. For instance:

- Lady Catherine de Bourgh is the guardian dragon of the treasure; the masculine, bossy, widowed aunt.
- Fitzwilliam Darcy is the saviour knight in shining armour who overcomes his enemies and rescues damsels in distress.
- George Wickham is the charming villain who shamelessly deceives and seduces the ladies and exploits the men; a wolf in sheep's clothing.
- Mrs Bennet is the brainless, attention-seeking woman who attracted a husband with her looks and does not know when to stop talking.
- Mr Bennet is the cynical, irresponsible father who will do anything for the sake of peace and entertainment.
- Mary Bennet is the humourless, unattractive, tedious 'bluestocking' who lives her life second-hand through books but is not as clever as she thinks.
- Lydia Bennet is the self-indulgent, wayward, selfish girl who thinks she knows best and causes lots of trouble for everyone else.
- Charlotte Lucas is the plain, pragmatic girl who is second choice but achieves her goal through sheer determination.
- Caroline Bingley is the bitchy, jealous rival who will do anything to get her man.

The Enlightenment

The Enlightenment was an important philosophical and intellectual eighteenth-century movement. It had many facets, but central was the primacy of critical intelligence and the importance of forming judgements based rigorously on evidence rather than relying on revelation (e.g. religion) or prejudice. The *Bildungsroman* (or novel of self-discovery through education and experience) was a characteristic Enlightenment form. Elizabeth has been described as exercising an 'Enlightenment scepticism' (Franco Moretti) in judging Darcy from evidence rather than taking him at face value.

PHILIP ALLAN LITERATURE GUIDE FOR A-LEVEL

Romanticism

The term 'Romantic', not actually coined until 1860, refers to the period of art, music and literature that falls roughly between 1775 and 1825. This period had a very different social and cultural focus from the preceding era of Swift, Johnson, Alexander Pope, Samuel Richardson, Laurence Sterne and Henry Fielding. Though Austen deals with social issues, she also looks at the causes and effects of behaviour arising from individual personality, which makes her proto-Romantic in that her plots derive as much from a character's choices and behaviour as from social imperatives. The proof of this is that no two of her characters are alike, and that many of them are complex and not easily pigeon-holed into one category. By including women as main characters to be reckoned with — and her women are not simply harridans, victims or ***femmes fatales*** — Austen reversed the practice of either ignoring or stereotyping women.

femme fatale
sensuous and alluring woman who seduces men

Romanticism's chief tenets were the importance of childhood, passion, the personal, love and Nature. Feelings are to be trusted rather than thoughts, and impulses followed rather than rules. Romantics champion rebellion, non-conformity and the cause of the lone individual against the system. They prefer to be outdoors and revere Nature as a divine force, believing that those who cut themselves off from their natural roots in the countryside will perish spiritually. Because of the inevitability of loss, pain, physical decay and old age — unless pre-empted by an early death — the Romantic mode is essentially a tragic one.

Austen's sympathies for Romantic characters and philosophies is, to say the least, limited: the traits of whimsy, affectation, egotism and self-indulgence are satirised (for instance in Isabella Thorpe in *Northanger Abbey* and Marianne Dashwood in *Sense and Sensibility*), and rebellious or radical traits are presented as dangerous to the community and to society as a whole (as illustrated by Frank Churchill in *Emma*). Elizabeth's breaking of convention and etiquette in going on foot through mud to Netherfield can only be condoned because of her concern for her sick sister and need to take on the parenting role because of the negligence of her mother, and we are given licence to support Elizabeth in her dirty petticoat because it is the unpleasant and jealous Miss Bingley who criticises her for it. Elizabeth also plays the Romantic heroine in being adamant that she will marry only for love; nonetheless, she must learn to moderate her liveliness with silence, and to curb her Romantic tendencies of secrecy, imagination, impulse and hasty judgement by the end of the novel. Austen's admired characters balance sense and sensibility in accordance with Aristotle's recipe of the

TASK 13

Which of the two central characters — Elizabeth and Darcy — do you consider to be more of an Enlightenment figure, or more of a Romantic figure? Or do they both contain elements of both philosophies? Prepare a balanced argument.

golden mean. However, they are Romantic in that they appreciate the countryside and dislike the town, and it is always in an urban context that unhappiness and decadent behaviour originate, as illustrated by Jane's trip to London and Lydia's to Brighton.

The rise of the novel

Novels were a comparatively late literary invention; the only prose that existed before the seventeenth century was in the form of sermons and improving moral tales. Prose, unlike drama and poetry, was not considered an appropriate medium for entertainment. A novel (or novella if relatively short) is defined as a fictional prose narrative having a plot that unfolds through the actions, speech and thoughts of its characters. Its origin is commonly associated with Daniel Defoe, who wrote *Robinson Crusoe* (1719) and *Moll Flanders* (1722).

By the late eighteenth century three-volume satirical, confessional and picaresque novels were well established, and romantic novels (in the sense of a love story rather than reflecting the Romantic movement) were appearing in response to an increasingly educated, middle-class, female readership in need of diversion, catered for by the invention of circulating lending libraries. Until the nineteenth century these novels were usually comic rather than tragic — the former being more palatable to the taste of the time — and often had a fashionable Gothic element, one associated with romance since the Middle Ages. For the first time female authors were being published, notable names being Fanny Burney (1752–1840) and Maria Edgeworth (1767–1849).

Epistolary novels

There was a vogue for epistolary novels in the eighteenth century still apparent in the works of Austen. *Pride and Prejudice* contains 21 letters printed in full and references to 44 letters, without which the plot could not function. Letters are particularly important in Chapters 48 and 49 when Lydia is being sought in London by Mr Gardiner and Mr Bennet, who need to report the developing situation to Longbourn. The tension builds up as the letters are anxiously awaited and delayed and the reader knows no more than the Bennet family.

Letters also enable characters to reveal secrets and convey their attitudes and personalities; sometimes they confirm what we already know about the letter-writer, as in the case of Mr Collins and Miss Bingley, but with the more complex characters letters can be a revelation, as with Darcy.

The epistolary mode is easily parodied for its lack of realism because letter writing seems an unlikely activity when the writer is physically or mentally traumatised. This, in addition to its lack of variety, was presumably a reason why the genre was fading when Austen was writing. Until her time epistolary novels were melodramatic and contained scenes of rape or seduction.

The letters, survivors from the earlier epistolary version, establish or develop character, plot, theme and style but their main function is to keep the reader informed of events. They also provide comedy, create tension and make moral points.

Many characters write or receive letters in the novel. Some are informative (like those of Mr and Mrs Gardiner), but others are written to interfere, demand or gloat (Mr Collins, Lydia, Mr Bennet), so that the character's purpose in writing reveals their type. The epistolary styles of Jane and Lydia, Mr Collins and Darcy, could not be more different and serve to distinguish admirable from reprehensible characters. Elizabeth is not a particularly active letter writer; the reader is made aware of her attitudes and behaviour through narrative. Austen uses letters to reveal the attitudes and behaviour of the other characters around her.

Most of the letters are in the second half of the novel, crossing physical divides and bridging gaps in knowledge and understanding. The biggest flurry of letters is caused by Lydia's misbehaviour, which implicates and draws in the extended Bennet and Darcy families, and both jeopardises and cements the relationship between Elizabeth and Darcy. Men were less commonly letter writers than women so it makes the situation of the elopement the more serious that the letters at this point are between father and uncle; these are practical, not social, missives.

Though some letters simply reinforce what we already know about the writer's personality, Darcy's letter to Elizabeth is crucial in allowing the reader — and its recipient — to become aware of a different character hidden beneath his social facade. Some critics maintain that Darcy's letter is unrealistic, contending that such a proud and reserved man would never reveal so many details of his private life. According to this view, the letter functions primarily as an artificial device through which Austen is able to introduce a large quantity of information while vindicating Darcy. One can argue, however, that the 'dreadful bitterness of spirit' in which Darcy claims to have written the letter explains its uncharacteristic nature.

Realism

One of the most radical features of the new novel genre was its attention to domestic and other detail. The aim was to convince

the reader of the specificity of the environment and the individual, whereas previous prose works deliberately presented a very general context, vague as to place and time and thus universally applicable. In attempting to describe human behaviour and surroundings, and to represent figures and objects exactly as they act or appear in life, Austen can be said to adhere much more to realism than did her predecessors Sterne or Fielding, or the female Gothic novelists. There is also a consciousness of duration of time and space (dates and places are very specific in *Pride and Prejudice*) and the use of convincing dialogue to show that she was aiming for veracity.

However, she uses fewer details of physical appearance than most of her contemporaries, much less description of decor and furniture and buildings, inside and out, and makes little mention of food. This has the effect of focusing the reader's attention on the abstract rather than the concrete; she mocks those of her characters who are only interested in domestic trivia and clothing.

Structure

The traditional dramatic device of a stranger arriving in town is the catalyst for various relationships and events to be set in motion. Starved of young men, the local community competes to attract the attentions of the newcomers. The expectation is that they will not be single for long, and that as they are in so much demand, they are likely to have more than one admirer and a choice of future partners. Since sanctioned meetings can only occur at balls and in drawing rooms, this is where the plot developments occur. Nearly all the events take place 'on stage' (with the exception of Lydia's elopement and its aftermath in London) and the reader goes where Elizabeth goes, so her visits to Kent, London and Derbyshire provide the movement of the novel.

The plot is generated by unforced character behaviour rather than by chance: Lydia's elopement; Mr Collins's proposal being refused by Elizabeth and accepted by Charlotte; Darcy's refusal to dance with Elizabeth at the Meryton Assembly; Lady Catherine's visit to Elizabeth. It is not easy to find an example of any event that is purely fortuitous, except for Darcy arriving early at Pemberley while Elizabeth is still in the vicinity, but even this can be attributed to his efficiency in wanting to prepare in advance for his guests. The duration of the novel is just over a year, from early autumn 1811 to late autumn 1812.

Pause for **Thought**

Do you consider that this is a 'realistic' novel? Find three ways in which it is, and three ways in which you consider it is not.

The plot is generated by…character behaviour rather than by chance

Delaying tactics

As in Shakespearean opening scenes, we first hear the main character discussed and disagreed over — and become aware of her being the favourite of one parent and not the other — before meeting her; this delaying tactic builds up expectation and interest, as does being told that 'Lizzy has something more of quickness than her sisters'.

One of Jane's letters from London is delayed so that two arrive together in Derbyshire and Elizabeth and the reader can be put in the picture in one go about the events concerning Lydia, which actually took place over several days, with a cumulative effect of disaster. Mr Gardiner's letter telling his brother-in-law that the situation has been resolved is also delayed, which causes the anxiety to be prolonged.

There is no reason for Bingley's delay in proposing to Jane, which requires him to visit Longbourn several times on his own, except that it serves to heighten the tension for the reader, the girls, and Mrs Bennet's nerves.

The three-volume novel

The reason the three-volume novel dominated the nineteenth century was that the only way a publisher could make a decent profit on books that appealed to the minority of people with the taste, education, and money for middle-class literary fare was to sell the text in three separate parts. Charles Mudie's circulating lending libraries created an expectation of three volumes of about 270 pages each, to be rented by the volume. This lengthy format affected all aspects of the content and structure of the late eighteenth- and nineteenth-century novel: copious dialogue, events and characters; many chapters; complex plot lines; and climax points at the end of each of the first two volumes.

By the end of Volume One of *Pride and Prejudice* all the characters have been introduced and their personalities, situations, aims and views made clear. That Elizabeth has just turned down Mr Collins and that Longbourn will therefore be lost makes the future look bleak for the Bennets at this point. Neither Jane nor Elizabeth have any marriage prospects, and their mother is frantic at her plans having all gone awry. Elizabeth's belief in Wickham and her determination to despise Darcy make it seem impossible to the reader that she could ever view Darcy in a better light.

Volume Two deals with the complications of Elizabeth's relationship with Darcy, but that of Bingley and Jane also deteriorates. The Rosings chapters expose Elizabeth to Darcy's aristocratic world and the failings of his aunt, which does nothing to make her think better of him. The

proposal therefore comes at a particularly inopportune moment. The reader is not surprised that Darcy is attracted to Elizabeth, because so many hints have been previously dropped, but Elizabeth is genuinely astonished and disturbed, and this makes the end of Chapter 42 dramatic, for 'To Pemberley, therefore, they were to go.' This could lead to embarrassing consequences, as could Lydia's ill-advised trip to Brighton as a camp-follower.

The resolution of Volume Three is entirely thanks to Darcy, who thus proves himself a hero after all. He impresses the Gardiners, whose opinion the reader and Elizabeth respect; he withdraws his objection and allows Bingley to propose to Jane; he saves Lydia and her family's reputation; he proves himself worthy of Elizabeth by having allowed himself to be humbled and taught a lesson by her; he is willing to go against his near relations in pursuing her and proposing to her again.

TASK **14**

Collect examples of characters who can be grouped in threes and events which occur three times.

Triple and dual structures

In addition to the overall structure being divided into three parts, and the triple syntactical structures used in the authorial style (see p. 71 of this guide), the novel also shows many other examples of being structured on a rule of three: Elizabeth receives three proposals; there are three eligible bachelors with whom her name is linked; there are three young ladies involved with Wickham; some events occur three times.

TASK **15**

Give examples of each of the dual structure features in pairings of: characters; rivalries; attitudes; letters; mirrored events.

There are also features of the novel which can be described as based on a dual system. Not only do some characters have a similar and/or opposite counterpart (see 'Pairs of characters', p. 50 of this guide) but the plot involves rivalries, conflicting attitudes, pairs of letters and mirrorings of events.

Language

Humour

Austen's novel is comic in the sense of containing humorous dialogue and amusing comments by the narrator and authorial voice, but she also uses humour as a weapon for character assassination, and as a means of raising serious concerns about behaviour and the suitability of relationships.

One of the ways of creating humour is to clash simple with complex characters. In each case there is a marked difference in speech styles between the pairs of characters and one character is allowed to be humorous at the expense of the other, who is made to look more insensitive and more foolish by the comparison.

- **Mrs Bennet and Mr Bennet:** She is made to seem ridiculous and he is made to seem witty; the marriage is thus established as an incompatible one.
- **Elizabeth and Mr Collins:** She strikes a blow for feminism in being more intelligent, rational and enlightened than him; he looks a fool for proposing to someone so unsuited to him and for continuing to pursue his case long after she has made her rejection clear.
- **Elizabeth and Lady Catherine:** The humour is ironic and the outcome of their verbal battle reverses normal expectations and those of Lady Catherine herself; her discomfiture is a come-uppance that the reader must enjoy, having endured so much of her previous pontificating.

Comic devices

Austen avoids all visual comedy devices in favour of caricature, witticisms, epigrams and the situational comedy device of bringing together characters of different intellect, class, gender or agenda to generate amusement and misunderstanding. In addition to Mr Collins and Lady Catherine, Lydia is dangerously close to being a caricature as her utterances rarely stray beyond soldiers, clothing and having a laugh. There is comedy in the use of bathetic juxtapositions by the narrator or heroine, as in the inference that the arrival of Lady Catherine can be compared to a pig getting into the garden, and that the time taken to stir a fire is the amount of time needed for a change of mind about whom one should marry.

Satire

Elizabeth owns up to laughing at the follies and vices of her acquaintances. Irony draws attention to folly, but satire goes further in being a deliberate, scathing attack with the aim of exposing to ridicule and contempt a type or an institution, and of pointing out the damage they cause to others.

The targets for satire in *Pride and Prejudice* are the clergy (Mr Collins); the aristocracy (Lady Catherine de Bourgh); social climbers (Sir William Lucas); irrational mothers (Mrs Bennet); negligent fathers (Mr Bennet). Jane and Bingley are gently mocked for their naivety, but they do not earn Elizabeth's or the reader's contempt. What distinguishes vice from folly is that it hurts others and is deliberate; Mrs Bennet is not educated, but Mr Collins is, and so is George Wickham. They should know better.

Wit

Austen claimed in a letter to her niece that 'Wisdom is better than wit, and in the long run will certainly have the laugh on her side', though her readers would disagree, since they read her for her wit rather than her wisdom. Elizabeth is actually punished for her wit and has learned the need to curb it by the end of the novel. Mr Bennet is the most guilty of employing wit, practised at the expense of his wife, silly daughters and cousin, but he is punished, at least briefly, by his conscience and the necessary intervention of others to sort out his youngest daughter's predicament; while he is amusing, he is not to be admired. On the other hand, those who are incapable of supplying or appreciating wit are presented as tedious; the important thing (and this lesson Elizabeth has to learn) is knowing when wit is, and is not, appropriate.

Serious humour

Because this is a didactic novel, even the most humorous passages have a serious message. The different layers of narrative in the novel create complex ironies, verbal and situational, which have a comic effect but which also make serious moral statements.

Mr and Mrs Bennet's conversation (Chapter 1)

This reveals their temperamental and intellectual incompatibility. We can immediately see the potential for Mrs Bennet being a cause of embarrassment and for Mr Bennet being neglectful of his responsibilities. Their conversation also highlights the faulty upbringing of their offspring, and what makes a good or bad choice of marriage partner.

Mr Collins's proposal to Elizabeth (Chapter 19)

Although hilarious, there are many serious underlying points being made here about the position of young women: the injustice of entailed estates; their captive position in having to suffer such approaches; their duty to their parents and not to their own feelings; the myth that women say 'no' when they mean 'yes'. Elizabeth is actually taking a huge risk in turning Collins down — as he tactlessly reminds her — and this evokes our admiration for her independent spirit.

...even the most humorous passages have a serious message

PHILIP ALLAN LITERATURE GUIDE **FOR A-LEVEL**

Dinner at Rosings (Chapter 29)

The laughable inquisition Lady Catherine subjects her guests to, and the discomfort she causes, break the rules of true hospitality. Her manners are far worse than those of the Gardiners, whom she despises as inferior; in this scene Austen is therefore making the point that the social hierarchy is fortuitous, not meritocratic, and is reversible.

Elizabeth's teasing of Jane (Chapter 59)

Elizabeth tells Jane that she fell in love with Darcy 'from my first seeing his beautiful grounds at Pemberley' (p. 353). This shockingly mercenary admission that she wants to be mistress of Pemberley can be dismissed as just teasing, but she is actually condemning the materialism involved in the choice of marriage partners and showing an understanding of the connection between houses and their owners. People may deceive, but houses do not.

Narrative modes

Austen's range and command of narrative modes enable her to create the dramatic and comic effects so appreciated by her fans. There are nine distinct narrative modes in her novels, and sometimes they merge into each other to convey even more complex effects. There are 26 speaking characters in *Pride and Prejudice* and they all have a recognisable and distinctive voice or **idiolect**. Because so much of the novel is in dialogue, most of which consists of sparring between two parties, the novel is dramatic and has therefore attracted many film makers.

1 Authorial voice

Often ironic, this differs from the narrative voice in being usually reflective and addressed directly to the reader. It is little used compared to other narrative modes, but memorable when it is. The opening sentence of the novel is clearly an opinion rather than objective narrative and it sets the tone for the novel: a mockery of the stereotype of mothers of daughters in general and of Mrs Bennet in particular. With hindsight it becomes doubly ironic; the cliché is shown to be a 'universal truth' by the eventual marriage of Mrs Bennet's three daughters, and she is proved right in thinking that Mr Bingley was in search of a wife.

The authorial voice is always obtrusive and occasionally clumsy. There is an awkward dismissiveness in the tone of 'It is not the object of this work to give a description of Derbyshire' and on p. 346, the authorial voice sounds bored, and even breaks the illusion of realism, as it reports that Darcy 'expressed himself on the occasion as sensibly and warmly as

idiolect style of speech peculiar to an individual character and recognisable as such

Taking it
Further

For a list of film and television productions of the novel, see p. 108 of this guide.

TASK 16

Watch one of the recent film or television adaptations and consider whether the visual presentation detracts from the primacy of dialogue in the written novel.

a man violently in love can be supposed to do'. At the beginning of the final chapter an authorial 'I' suddenly intrudes in 'I wish I could say…'.

The paragraph on p. 240 beginning 'There was certainly at this moment…' is a good example of a passage in which it is impossible to differentiate between Elizabeth's, the narrator's and the authorial voice, for instance the sudden rhetorical question: 'What praise is more valuable than the praise of an intelligent servant?'

Mr Bennet's mode in particular is like that of the author, ironic and epigrammatic (e.g. 'In such cases, a woman has not often much beauty to think of') and this is what endears him to us as readers, but equally misleads us into thinking that he has the author's approval. Elizabeth has inherited his ironic view of life and style of speech (which is what also endears her to us) but it misleads her into thinking that she has a sound basis for judgement.

2 Objective narrative

This voice sets the scene, explains the circumstances and introduces characters. It is a literary convention that we always believe factual information and statements made by the narrative voice. However, Austen inserts value judgements and opinions of characters as well as facts into this apparently objective mode, which means we must guard against being misled. There is an ironic reference to Mrs Bennet as 'his lady' on the first page that is clearly not simply a factual label for the unladylike wife of Mr Bennet, though it purports to be so. There are passages, such as the long paragraph on p. 17, which begin as objective narrative but which seamlessly slide into authorial voice; we are told that the Bingley sisters 'were in the habit of spending more than they ought, and of associating with people of rank; and were therefore in every respect entitled to think well of themselves, and meanly of others'. The beginning of this quotation is factual but the word 'therefore' signals the ironic comment to come.

Nearly all the final chapter, summing up the future for each of the main characters, is delivered in the objective narrative voice. It is also used to tell us things that Elizabeth cannot know, such as Charlotte's 'scheme' to win Mr Collins for herself by setting out to meet him 'accidentally', on p. 119.

3 Coloured narrative

Some of the narrative is delivered directly by Elizabeth, unmediated by the objective narrative voice. This is necessary to enable the reader to be deceived, along with the heroine, to create dramatic effect and to engineer a denouement. However, it also has a moral purpose in showing the reader, rather than just telling us, how easy it is to be taken in by someone we like and think we can trust. This mode is used by Austen more than objective narrative; Darcy, Mr Bennet, Jane, Bingley, the Gardiners, and Mrs Reynolds must all be agreed with by the reader at times. However, the coloured narrative mode demands provisional assent from the reader because we like and wish to empathise with Austen's attractive main character and share her enjoyment of the follies of others; we are therefore carried along and tricked into thinking she is offering objective judgement on Wickham and Darcy, especially as Elizabeth is right about all the other characters. This amalgam of narrator and heroine makes the reader identify closely with the latter and uncritically accept the feelings and views that she delivers with the authority of objective narrative.

Coloured narrative is also used to convey the collective thoughts of the community (as on p. 12: 'What a contrast between him and his friend!' and on p. 13: 'the proudest, most disagreeable man in the world') and links with the free indirect speech mode (see number 8 below) as such comments capture the expression of the gossip going around.

4 Character voice: dialogue

This mode constitutes the majority of the book, with coloured narrative coming second; the content of the novel is in fact around 90% dialogue. The purpose and effect of this narrative mode is to allow characters to reveal themselves entertainingly through the content and style of their speech, and it has the advantage of economy in that two or more characters can do so simultaneously, allowing the reader can judge them without any need of help from the narrative voice.

...the content of the novel is in fact around 90% dialogue

What characters say is much more revealing of their beliefs and morals than any physical description can be. Those who are unwilling or unable to engage in genuine conversation, such as Mr Bennet, Mary, Lady Catherine and the early Darcy, can also be judged accordingly. Since the majority of dialogue necessarily takes the form of question and answer, characters can elicit information from each other on behalf of the reader.

As pairs or groups Austen's characters perform as if on stage, and in ever-changing combinations. This semi-formal mode of semi-public conversation has rules of engagement, so that characters can be judged by how well they adhere to them; Mr Collins and Lady Catherine fail by being too verbose and too domineering respectively, and too self-regarding jointly. There is not only a variety of finely distinguished voices to be heard, but the dramatic effect of immediacy is created.

Furthermore, dialogue provides scope for irony to function, as characters can convey the opposite impression to that which they intend, as well as reveal that they know less than the reader, creating dramatic irony.

Dialogue advances the action and set pieces of disagreement can be aired, such as that between Charlotte and Elizabeth on the subject of marriage, and between Darcy and Elizabeth on women's education. It has been noted that dialogue is not used for intimate moments, as the author is more comfortable in social rather than private mode. Once couples have reached an understanding, exchanges between them serve no further purpose, and scenes of passion are avoided.

5 Character voice: talking to oneself

Characters sometimes talk to themselves in direct speech. There is an example on p. 182 where Elizabeth is reliving the previous conversation with Colonel Fitzwilliam and her speech functions as the answer to him that she did not give at the time, and as her attempt to convince herself that Darcy's pride is of the 'worst kind'.

Her reaction to Darcy's letter in Chapter 36 takes the same form of her 'repeatedly exclaiming, "This must be false!"' (p. 198), and on pp. 201–02 she talks to herself for a whole paragraph to show the extent of her mental disturbance and feeling of humiliation. She talks, apparently aloud, to herself again in the opening of Chapter 54, until Jane arrives. Thoughts are also indicated by speech marks, as on p. 212 when Elizabeth reacts to Lydia's plan to go to Brighton, and presumably her speech on p. 322 is made internally, since she is in public. In each case the turmoil of Elizabeth's mind or dislike of something is conveyed by this method.

6 Character voice: written speech

Letters are another mode of direct speech which allow characters to speak uninterrupted for much longer than would be considered realistic or polite in conversation. The reader can appreciate the situation of the writer but is positioned alongside the letter's recipient. We can imagine and empathise with how they are feeling while reading it, and before we are told by the narrator how to respond. This is especially true when Elizabeth is reading her long letter from Darcy.

7 Character voice: speech within speech

Though not widely used, one example occurs on p. 103 when Mr Collins is telling Elizabeth his reasons for marrying and in doing so quotes the instruction of Lady Catherine to find 'an active, useful sort of person' to marry. It enables both characters to be mocked simultaneously, her for saying such things and him for agreeing with them; the doubling of silly

...dialogue is not used for intimate moments

voices adds to the comic effect, and allows us to see similarities between the quoter and the quoted, as when Mrs Bennet tells us what her sister, Mrs Philips, said.

8 Character voice: free indirect speech

This hybrid style of third person narration combines the characteristics of reported speech with those of direct speech. Passages written using free indirect speech are often ambiguous as to whether they convey the views of the narrator or of the character the narrator is describing, creating an ironic interaction between internal and external perspectives. This device, which later came to be known as *style indirect libre*, is particularly associated with Austen's narrative technique, whereby the actual words a character speaks are incorporated into the narrative without inverted commas. The character's speech habits can be mocked in this way, as their expression is so readily identifiable within the more elegant and competent surrounding narrative style.

9 Character voice: incorporated speech

Austen sometimes quotes in speech marks part of the direct speech made by a character in an earlier conversation, allowing the reader to hear things that they were not privy to earlier. This device has the effect of doubling the time frame without losing the immediacy of it being the first time of utterance, as the earlier effect on the interlocutor can be imagined. Taken out of context these remarks can be made to seem silly or trivial, or to take on a gravity equal to a quotation from an authority figure, depending on character and context. There is an example on p. 182 where Colonel Fitzwilliam is echoed in Elizabeth's review of the earlier conversation.

Language use in the Regency period

English language and usage has changed in various ways since the late eighteenth century. Some of these changes are easy to spot, particularly those to do with syntax and punctuation (especially the abundance of commas) and spelling (Austen consistently spelt 'chuse', 'stile' and 'develope' thus, and words we now spell with 'ie' appear as 'ei', e.g. 'neice' and 'freindship'). The capitalisation of abstract nouns seems a trivial difference but was important in that such words as 'Evil', 'Honour', 'Principle' and 'Vice' stand out as having biblical connotations, and they therefore carry moral approbation or condemnation. Changes in the meanings of words are harder to identify and for that reason can mislead the reader into missing signs or wrongly interpreting them. Some of these are dealt with below.

It was a convention of the period to use fictitious place names for all but the major towns, and to leave blanks for some other proper names (e.g. on p. 72). On p. 211 there are blanks for both a town in Hertfordshire and the name of Wickham's regiment. London, Bath and Brighton, however, are large enough be mentioned without fear of giving offence to any particular group of people. It was also common for dates to be left incomplete in contemporary novels; blanks fostered the illusion that the privacy of real people was being protected.

There is little use of language that could be called lyrical or poetic, whereas there are many examples of typically eighteenth-century prose and essay devices, such as **aphorism** and **antithesis**, which Austen gives to her favoured characters: e.g. 'One has got all the goodness, and the other all the appearance of it' (Elizabeth, p. 217) and '*his* perfect indifference, and *your* pointed dislike, make it so delightfully absurd!' (Mr Bennet p. 344). In a letter to Cassandra, Austen referred to 'the playfulness & Epigrammatism of the general stile' of *Pride and Prejudice*.

aphorism a terse statement embodying a general truth or acknowledged opinion, e.g. 'mediocrity is forgiven more easily than talent'

antithesis

contrasting ideas by balancing words or phrases of opposite meaning, e.g. 'her jealousy and dislike of one sister much exceeded her affection for the other'

Changed meanings

Certain key adjectives are used frequently in the novel. For example, 'proper', 'just' and 'serious' do not seem particularly 'loaded' now, but for Austen they indicated acceptable social behaviour and moral worth. Likewise, words such as 'giddy' or 'silly' may seem harmless or even attractively childlike to a modern reader, but in fact these words then meant being deficient in consideration and moderation.

The following words have also changed their meaning, are no longer in current use, or carried more moral weight than nowadays.

Elegant

This word is usually used in a critical sense to mean vain, and is often applied to women, particularly Londoners, who think too much of fashion and who try too hard to impress, such as Caroline Bingley. Mr Collins accuses Elizabeth of being an 'elegant female', which he implicitly defines as possessing 'affectation and coquetry' (p. 107). However, the word also appears in the novel in reference to someone's principles and manners rather than to their appearance. True elegance is of the mind and is a goal to be aspired to; it is the opposite of vulgarity.

Sensibility

This can be defined as sentimental and emotional indulgence. The modern equivalent would be sensitivity, generally regarded now as a desirable trait, at least in moderate amounts. As an opposite of 'sense', however, it is seen as suspect in Austen's characters. The desire to prove their sensibility (i.e. delicacy of feeling) is what led women to faint at the drop of a hat and thus demonstrate their ladylike fragility during the decades that followed.

Austen presents common sense and sound judgement as more worthy attributes than over-refined emotions, as sentimentality and emotional self-indulgence were considered dangerous and likely to lead to excess, error and other moral dangers.

Vulgar

Meaning literally 'of the crowd', this did not have the modern meaning of gross or rude, but was still a damaging assessment to make of someone, the equivalent of calling them 'common'. Mrs Bennet and her younger daughters are judged to be vulgar by the Bingley sisters and Lady Catherine, and rightly so, but Mrs Bennet's elder daughters and brother are less so than those who judge.

Gentleman

Originally meaning refined and courteous, 'gentil' evolved into the English word 'gentle', and the French and Italian words for 'kind'. It was used in Austen's time to denote someone belonging to the class of 'gentleman', one that was very important to her and to her characters. Darcy is horrified by Elizabeth's accusation that his conduct is unbecoming of a gentleman, and she makes a point of telling Lady Catherine that she is a 'gentleman's daughter'.

❮ Top ten *quotation*

Gentle manners and behaviour were thought to be the product of noble birth and what distinguished the higher from the lower classes; however, Austen makes it clear that these qualities are a matter of upbringing and not of blood.

Duty

Duty (usually capitalised in Austen) conferred an obligation on a par with a religious imperative. Lady Catherine appeals to duty as a reason why Elizabeth cannot be allowed to marry her nephew. Duty to family was paramount and unquestioned, as was duty to hosts and guests, and an extension of the concept of duty was that of gratitude, which Mr Collins expects to be shown by the Bennets for his condescension in trying to marry one of the daughters to offset the entail. Darcy continues to do his duty by Wickham, long after he would wish to have nothing more to do with him, because the bond between their fathers obliges him to.

The social hierarchy of the period, descended from the feudal system, was only operable because everyone knew their place and did their duty, upwards and downwards. Elizabeth is also conscious of a duty to herself, which is why, unlike Charlotte, she will not agree to become the wife of Mr Collins, though this means overriding her duty to her parents. Fortunately her father relieves her of this obligation by saying he would disown her if she wanted to marry Mr Collins.

Typical aspects of Austen's language

TASK 17

Find five examples of adverbial intensifiers and analyse their effect on the reader.

Adverbial intensifiers

The adverbs of degree (e.g. 'extremely', 'exceedingly') are used to reveal self-indulgence and lack of control of thought, emotion and deed; they are symptomatic of a lack of moderation and restraint. In Austen's world view, extreme and inconcise expression is indicative of uncontrolled and rebellious tendencies that can lead to political revolution and chaos, the end of the old order, tradition and conservatism. Lydia, a breaker of rules, is at fault in this respect, as is her mother; Mrs Bennet favours the intensifier 'so' in front of adjectives even when she is not making a comparison, as in 'so pleased', 'so happy', 'so handsome', 'so tall'. Superlatives and hyperbole indicate a jumping to conclusions and error of judgement, as in 'He was the proudest, most disagreeable man in the world.'

Question marks, exclamations and dashes

Characters whose speech is dotted with attention-seeking question and exclamation marks are shown to be overdramatic and prone to showing off, as well as to be revealing lack of previous reflection on their utterances. Mrs Bennet's speech at the bottom of p. 43, which includes dashes as well as exclamations and questions, shows a sloppiness and want of syntactical organisation that, by definition, gives the impression of casual rather than sophisticated speech. Lydia's rambling monologue on pp. 213–14 is not only full of grammatical errors, exaggerations and vulgar expressions (such as 'Lord!' and 'you can't think') but also consists entirely of names and exclamations (and simple or compound sentences). Kitty uses the exclamatory monosyllable 'La!' as an affectation.

The fact that Darcy's letter in Chapter 35 contains so many dashes (and so many sentences beginning with 'But') can only be explained by his being in a highly perturbed state and unable, for once, to collect and organise his thoughts and his syntax. The effect is to show the reader and Elizabeth a very different Darcy, and to signal that he will be less reserved in the second half of the novel. The dashes become fewer as the letter progresses, however, as if he has become calmer with the writing of it.

Triple syntactical structures

'She was a woman of mean understanding, little information, and uncertain temper' (Chapter 1). This description of Mrs Bennet as a list of three adjective/noun phrases was considered the elegant way to construct sentences and the rule of three was applied to single words, phrases or clauses. The author and her intelligent, educated or socially superior characters speak in triples: Elizabeth laments that Darcy should stoop to 'such malicious revenge, such injustice, such inhumanity' towards 'the godson, the friend, the favourite of his father' (p. 79), describes Bingley as 'sweet tempered, amiable, charming' (p. 81), and attacks Darcy for telling her that he likes her 'against your will, against your reason, and even against your character' (p. 186). Mrs Gardiner says 'so hackneyed, so doubtful, so indefinite' (p. 138) and 'a violation of decency, honour, and interest' (p. 268); Mr Gardiner describes Darcy as 'perfectly well behaved, polite and unassuming' (p. 246); even Lady Catherine threatens that Elizabeth 'will be censured, slighted, and despised' (p. 336) for being 'a young woman without family, connections, or fortune' (p. 337) who refuses 'to obey the claims of duty, honour, and gratitude' (p. 338). It is because Wickham can adopt this measured, sophisticated and argumentatively powerful style that he deceives Elizabeth and the reader.

Concrete and domestic nouns

Polite and educated discourse consisted of discussion of ideas rather than objects, especially not things of a mundane and domestic nature, which included servants, and particularly not when dancing. Instead the abstract nouns of morality — such as sense, courage, fortitude, vanity, folly, reason — were unashamedly and continually discussed to raise the tone of conversation. Mr Collins peppers his pontificating pronouncements with self-aggrandising abstracts but ruins the effect by descending into prosaic details of the decor at Rosings (such as its £800 chimney-piece), which reveals his spiritual poverty as surely as certain members of the Bennet family reveal theirs through talk of bonnets, barouches, and the colour of Wickham's coat. Lydia is more concerned about her wedding clothes than her choice of husband or her reputation, and instructs Harriet Forster to instruct the servant Sally to mend the slit in her muslin gown (a symbol if ever there was one).

Non-sentences, simple sentences

Mrs Bennet is the main offender against sentence construction. On p. 14 she cannot form a complex sentence, as shown by the frequent semi-colons and her reliance on 'and' as a connective. Her speech on the next page includes 'excessively', a common cant intensifier, and exclamations, non-sentences and hyperbolic language: 'never in my life', 'horrid' and 'detest'. On p. 357 she is barely able to form a sentence of any kind. Lydia also has her mother's syntactical weaknesses.

Idiolects

Most novelists distinguish between class and gender in terms of topic of conversation, but few go in for Austen's subtle gradations and idiosyncrasies in the speech of individual characters. Though we cannot know the standards of normal speech before the invention of the tape recorder, we can know from intratextual comparison whether a character is to be considered affected, pompous, natural, vulgar, etc. The whole range of dialect and accented popular speech is excluded so the scale is narrow, but this allows for fine distinctions within moderately educated speech and polite conversation, so that every nuance and deviation is indicative of attitude and moral status.

Bingley accuses Darcy of using 'words of four syllables', which reflects the latter's intellectual habits and lack of ease in speech, the opposite of his friend's mode of conversing. Mr Collins uses clichés that reveal his shallowness, insensitivity to language and lack of creativity; he is a man who refuses to read novels. His use of **litotes**, e.g. 'will not fail of being acceptable' (p. 106) and 'not disagreeably' (p. 208), and prolix, convoluted sentences is evidence of his pomposity.

TASK *18*

Collect examples of the idiolects of the principal characters. You could then see whether other students can identify the speaker from their style alone.

litotes a deliberate understatement, often used for ironic or comic effect

Images and symbols

In addition to reinforcing themes, imagery gives atmosphere, pattern, integrity and meaning to a text, and can help to delineate character. Symbols represent abstract concepts greater than themselves.

Eyes/view

Seeing and being seen was an essential part of the actual and moral life of the times. It is also part of the novel's narrative approach to play ironically with viewpoint, and this image is related to the themes of judgement and prejudice (i.e. a partial view). 'View' is used to mean prospect and outlook, applied both to the countryside and houses, as well as attitude and judgement. The two meanings are connected to the imagery of eyes and reflection, itself an ambiguous word, and these all come together in the context of Elizabeth's visit to Pemberley and the views and visions she encounters there.

Pictures

In a pre-photographic world a picture meant a portrait or landscape painting, when this was the only way of creating a likeness. It is also used as an idiom to mean forming an impression of a character, as in the dialogue between Elizabeth and Darcy:

> **'…I could wish, Miss Bennet, that you were not to sketch my character at the present moment, as there is reason to fear that the performance would reflect no credit on either.'**

> **'But if I do not take your likeness now, I may never have another opportunity' (p. 92).**

Elizabeth falls in love with Darcy's picture on the wall at Pemberley, as well as with his likeness to the well-cultivated and aesthetically tasteful estate that belongs to him and therefore reflects him. To look as pretty as a picture was an ideal of the period, on the basis of which all costume and activity was predicated; everything must look attractive and posed, as in the movements and symmetry of the style of dancing. This is why Elizabeth's muddy petticoat is criticised by the Bingley sisters, who care only about appearances and superficialities, and why everyone is taken in by the picturesque Wickham in his colourful coats. The redcoats are all 'dangerous' to dizzy, young, men-starved girls who fall for the idea of a soldier and chase them, forgetting moral proprieties, as Lydia and Kitty do. They discuss whether Wickham will be wearing his red or his blue coat, as if this is more important than his character. The community generally is pleased to have the redcoats billeted there to liven up the social scene and provide potential husbands, not considering the possible less desirable consequences for their daughters.

Schemes

A much-used word in the novel, 'scheme' carried more menace then than it does now. The original schemer was Satan — plotting first against God and then Adam and Eve in the Garden of Eden — and so, like 'evil', the use of the word 'scheme' is forceful when used in the work of an author who rarely used strong language of any kind and regarded it as an impropriety in her characters. A schemer is devious, dishonourable and untrustworthy. Caroline Bingley schemes against Elizabeth and Jane in

her pursuit of Darcy; Wickham schemes to marry a woman with money; Lydia plots the 'delicious scheme' (p. 212) of going off to Brighton; Mr Collins arrives at Longbourn with a scheme to marry one of the Bennet daughters; Lady Catherine's impromptu visit to Longbourn is a 'scheme'. No schemer is successful or to be admired in Austen, as by definition a scheme involves secrecy and manipulation of others.

Performances

'The power of doing anything with quickness is always much prized by the possessor, and often without any attention to the imperfection of the performance' (pp. 47–48). Simply being in public demands a performance, and most of the time Austen's characters are being watched, not just when dancing, singing, playing an instrument or a game but when sitting, walking, talking and in every aspect of their daily lives conducted in public. Their parlours are the stage for the entrances and exits for the multitude of daily visitors, and their costumes are carefully designed with the aim of cutting a fine figure (Caroline Bingley walks around the room in a performance designed to allow Darcy to appreciate hers).

Conversations were also planned and even rehearsed, and not only by Mr Collins; Mr Bennet and Mary deliver all of their utterances as *bons mots* to be appreciated by their audiences. Austen is suspicious of performers who are too adept at acting convincingly (like Wickham) or have a self-dramatising theatrical tendency (like Mrs Bennet), as neither can be presumed to be capable of genuine feeling. The word 'performance', however, disappears from the novel after Elizabeth has read Darcy's letter; they are no longer playing a part and hiding behind a mask.

Symbolic events

Balls are *par excellence* social events intended to give enjoyment, so when Elizabeth receives a snub at the Meryton assembly it has the shock factor of at least a slap across the face because the disappointment she experiences is in a context of pleasure for everyone else, especially Jane.

Elizabeth arriving at Netherfield with mud on her petticoat is a symbolic moment in the novel, revealing and representing far more than the fact itself. It shows the superficiality of the etiquette of the Bingley sisters — who are not truly refined or they would not embarrass a guest by drawing attention to her condition — and at the same time the genuine affection of Elizabeth for her sister in being brave enough to undertake a journey on foot and in the rain, no ordinary matter in those days and likely to result in more damage to the health than a soiled undergarment.

...most of the time Austen's characters are being watched

To Darcy it symbolises that she is a passionate woman, different from the doll-like creatures he is surrounded by; his interest is sparked by her dramatic entry.

The main symbol in the novel is Pemberley, which reflects its owner, revealing the hidden and worthy side of his character and how those who really know him feel about him, and represents the importance to England of tradition, history and country life.

The main symbol in the novel is Pemberley

The significance of locations

For Austen, places usually meant houses; the events in her novels take place almost exclusively indoors. Houses reveal their owners not so much because they indicate social status, though they do, but because how they are managed exemplifies moral status. Austen is vague about the designs and amount of accommodation, however, since, as with her characters, the tendency is towards the delineation of the type rather than the particular, in order for them to be more representative.

Longbourn

Longbourn is the name of both the house and the village in Hertfordshire of which the Bennets 'were the principal inhabitants'. It would not be possible to draw a plan of Longbourn (either house or village), although so much of the novel takes place there. However, we do know that it has a shrubbery 'hermitage', and that Mr Bennet has a library. Jane and Elizabeth share a bedroom, but there is room to put up Mr Collins when he visits them, suggesting perhaps six bedrooms, including the servant's. Mrs Bennet mentions a female servant called Hill. They have a coach and two horses, but the latter are sometimes lent out to a local farmer so transport is not always available to them (hence the excuse for Jane being stranded at Netherfield). Mr Collins is pleased to have a claim to the house, whose estate is worth £2,000 a year.

London

The London area had over a million inhabitants, and was several times larger than any other city in Britain. Big cities, particularly London and the fashionable spa town of Bath, are the venue for decadence, shame, unkindness and unhappiness in all Austen's novels, and associated with loose morals in high society. Mr Bennet is forced to travel to London to try to sort out Lydia's social suicide in running off there, unmarried, with Wickham. Darcy owns a house in London, but does not seem to choose to spend much time in it. London represents fashion and snobbery; exactly where one lived in London was an important indicator of social status.

Brighton

Austen knew about the fashionable south-coast seaside resort of Brighton because her brother Henry was stationed there after becoming a militiaman on the outbreak of hostilities with France in February 1793. Brighton was notorious as a place of recreation and ostentation, and was associated with the licentious behaviour of the Prince Regent and his decadent coterie. It is an unwise trip to Brighton that brings about the opportunity and moral context for Lydia's downfall.

Rosings

This grand edifice is situated in Kent, another of the home counties, and is the residence of the widow, Lady Catherine de Bourgh, and her daughter Anne. At nearby Hunsford Mr Collins lives in the rectory with his newly acquired and recently impregnated wife, Charlotte. Being invited to dine at Rosings is the highest honour imaginable for the sycophantic vicar, and he enjoys showing off this patronising privilege to the rest of the Lucas family and Elizabeth when they visit. The furniture is showy and tasteless, and Elizabeth is oppressed by being there. Rosings estate is fenced by palings, which form a barrier representing the social exclusivity their owner believes in.

Chatsworth House in Derbyshire, which might have been one of the sources for Pemberley; its garden design marries apparently wild nature and ordered classicism

Hunsford

The vicarage is an adjunct to Rosings Park, physically and socially, but distinctly separated from it by palings, symbolising both the acolyte role of the incumbent vicar and his clearly defined inferior status. Charlotte has tried to make it homely, with her poultry, but her husband wants to show it off to visitors as a superior residence.

Derbyshire

Although not particularly far north geographically, Derbyshire was distant enough from Hertfordshire in a time of limited travel to count as another country for Elizabeth, one offering new views and perspectives on life in general, and hers in particular. It has hills and lakes and open vistas different from Hertfordshire, offering Elizabeth literally new prospects and attractions. The rugged terrain symbolises Romanticism and it is therefore appropriate that it is there that Elizabeth becomes truly acquainted with the longing of her heart, a need for escape and a desire for independence.

Pemberley

Elizabeth does not recognise the true Darcy until she has seen his house. Commentators claim that her remark to her sister about when she first knew she was in love with him must be teasing or ironic, which it obviously is on one level, but in fact it can also be taken straightforwardly to mean that the 'correlation between the moral and the material' (Eagleton), between him and his house, is the final proof she needs that Darcy is the perfect gentleman and the right one for her. When Lady Catherine asks whether 'the shades of Pemberley' are to be polluted by her being connected to the Darcy family, she makes it sound as though Elizabeth is the serpent about to destroy the Garden of Eden. The language is ridiculously bombastic, because classical and extreme, and the ridicule rebounds upon the speaker, but the point is still being made that Pemberley represents paradise. Darcy appears out of the ground like a *genius loci*, at one with his property, a genial host and an almost unrecognisably amiable entity; such is the power of place and the idea of home. Darcy is Pemberley, and Elizabeth yearns for both. Uncomfortable in drawing rooms, Darcy can now be seen and appreciated in his natural surroundings and true element, in which he can talk about fishing.

The interior of the house is also described in terms that could be applied to its owner: 'well-proportioned', 'handsome', 'real elegance'. The description of Pemberley is an example of the eighteenth-century tradition of 'moralized landscape design in which an appropriate balance of nature and art, beauty and its use is the sign of a properly responsible moral outlook' (note 2 on p. 430 of the Penguin edition). Not the apparel but the architecture, grounds and decor proclaim the man.

TASK *19*

Collect evidence from the novel to support the assertion that places were important to Austen and her characters.

Taking it *Further*

Read N. Onyett's article 'Location, location, location', about the importance of the houses in *Pride and Prejudice* (*English Review*, Vol. 19, No. 3, February 2009, pp. 2–5).

Contexts

Biographical context

For a timeline of Austen's life and works, see the downloads on the free website at **www.philipallan.co.uk/literatureguidesonline**.

The Austen family

Austen's father, the Reverend George Austen, was a vicar in the Church of England. Jane, born in 1775, was the seventh of eight children (six boys and two girls) all of whom, unusually for that period, survived to adulthood. Her only sister, Cassandra, was three years older. As with the Brontë sisters, a clergyman father offered his daughters the opportunity to be considered gentry despite limited means; they could also expect to be educated beyond the station of most women of the time, just as education had elevated their fathers. There were always books to be found in a vicarage that would not otherwise have been readily available, and a habit of study to go with them.

> ...a clergyman father offered... the opportunity to be considered gentry despite limited means

The young Jane nearly died of a fever while away at school, and she returned home with Cassandra when she was nine and was thereafter educated by her parents. Jane was devoted to and influenced by Cassandra, and like her she never married, though four of her five brothers did. It is believed that Cassandra may well have influenced Jane's rejection of her one offer of marriage in order to keep her sister to herself. Of her brothers, one, Francis, rose in the navy from midshipman to admiral, and another brother, James, was a published writer in his own magazine, *The Loiterer*. Austen's father encouraged his daughter's literary aspirations, ensuring that she always had writing paper, which was then an expensive luxury item.

Austen's nephew James Edward Austen-Leigh, who wrote about her in 1870, tells us that according to family recollections Jane met in a southern seaside town a clergyman whom she might have married if he had not died. Cassandra was betrothed to a reverend who died of yellow fever in the West Indies in 1797, so Jane was copying her sister's experience in this as in so much else. At Christmas in 1796 Jane met Tom Lefroy, her 'Irish friend', with whom she fell in love. He admitted as an old man and as Lord Chief Justice of Ireland that he had loved her too.

In 1802 Cassandra and Jane returned to Steventon, now held as a living by James. Harris Bigg-Wither, son of a neighbouring county family, there proposed to Jane, who accepted but then had doubts and changed her mind overnight. She thus became one of the most famous maiden aunts in English history.

Austen's letters

Cassandra and Jane sent letters every three or four days when they were apart, and always had one on the go. Readers of Austen's novels have sometimes been surprised and even shocked to discover the acerbity of the wit of her letters, which often mock an acquaintance in vitriolic and unfair ways (e.g. 'his legs are too short, and his tail too long'). The full evidence of this side of her was censored by Cassandra, who destroyed all but 168 of Jane's letters to protect her sister's reputation; she removed everything intimate about family or lovers, and thereby everything which could satisfy public curiosity about her sister, unfortunately leaving the impression that Austen was dedicated to trivia and gossip.

Austen's death

By the time Austen broke off from writing *Sanditon* in March 1817, after 12 chapters, she was seriously ill with an unknown illness, possibly cancer or Addison's disease. She went to lodge in Winchester two months later in order to be near her doctor. She died in Cassandra's arms a few weeks later at the age of 41 and at the height of her powers. Though this was not considered a particularly young age to die at the time (and the Brontë family fared far worse), Austen's sister lived to be 70 and her brother the admiral reached the age of 91.

Religion and morality

Though much was made of her piety after her death, Austen does not overtly refer to religion in her work; no one prays or has an inner spiritual struggle, and God is rarely mentioned. However, the Christian precepts of neighbourliness, charity, patience and justice inform the decent social behaviour of every approved-of character in her works as a form of secularised Christianity to be applied to fellow humans.

There is little scene-setting and material detail in her works, but there is a fidelity to the niceties of social interaction and mimetic realism of speech within the closed world that she is describing and assessing; these niceties have been described as 'the long shadows of small events in a limited society'. Through what Hough (*Selected Essays*, 1978, p. 227)

…the Christian precepts of neighbourliness, charity, patience and justice inform…decent social behaviour

calls 'strongly ideological constructions', 'coherence is attained by a deliberate limitation of possibilities', creating a distinctive moral system still recognised today, and actually still practised until at least the First World War. Eagleton comments on 'her extraordinary moral intelligence' in *The English Novel: An Introduction* (2005, pp. 94–122).

Literary influences

Austen was allowed the uncensored use of the 500 volumes in her father's library, and read Samuel Richardson's *Sir Charles Grandison* as a child. She was particularly fond of this work, and Isabella Thorpe's condemnation of it in *Northanger Abbey* as 'an amazing horrid book' is major evidence of Isabella's lack of literary taste. In Richardson's novel there are descriptions of sisters, and particularly one called Charlotte, who could be a prototype for the heroine of *Pride and Prejudice* in being high-spirited, teasing, captivating, lively, articulate and arch, with a badly behaved father. There are also other character types and concerns that are reflected in Austen's novel, including a fortune-hunting army officer, 'girls of slender fortunes', and many discussions of love and marriage.

According to Henry, his sister Jane was a precocious reader and 'intimately acquainted with the merits and defects of the best essays and novels in the English language'. He stated in his biographical note that Johnson and Cowper were her favourite 'moral writers'. She admired Johnson's *Rasselas* and his essays in the *Rambler* and the *Idler*, allowing his ironic and measured style to influence her own. Cowper's long poem 'The Task' condemned field sports and their cruelty, but because her brothers were so fond of them Austen never openly condemns them in her fiction or surviving letters. She also kept quiet on politics and women's rights (Mary Wollstonecraft's *Vindication of the Rights of Woman* was published to a furore Austen could not have been unaware of in 1792). It seems her staunch Tory background silenced her possible sympathies towards radical sentiments, which she did not dare to endorse publicly out of loyalty to her family and fear of the effect it would have on her literary standing. However, she discreetly satirises hunters and male chauvinists through uncharitable portraits such as that of John Thorpe in *Northanger Abbey*, and her books quietly insist on and illustrate the moral and intellectual parity of the sexes.

> …her books quietly insist on and illustrate the moral and intellectual parity of the sexes

Although place is important to Austen, as represented in three of her seven novel titles (including *Sanditon*), another three are moral titles; at a time when it was common to choose eponymous titles (i.e. the same as the name of the main character), as Fielding and Richardson did, *Emma* is the only name Austen uses as a title.

We know from C. Tomalin (*Jane Austen*, 2000, p. 67) that Austen enjoyed Sterne's playful exposure of literary convention and artifice, and despite not particularly approving of the content of Fielding's works, Austen's own satiric manner of mocking absurdity and pricking pretentiousness owes something to him. Her novels reflect the social attitudes of the females of the upper bourgeoisie of her time, but look backward to the stylistic imperatives and moral absolutes of Dr Johnson and the Augustan period of the mid-eighteenth century, the only certainties in a frighteningly revolutionary age when so much else was in a state of flux or dispute.

Literary career

Jane started writing as a child, but of her surviving juvenilia *Love and Freindship* (sic), written when she was 15 and dedicated to her elder cousin Eliza, is probably the best known. Although she had been writing since the age of 12, Austen's first published work came at the age of 35, and only four of her novels were published in her lifetime — *Sense and Sensibility* (1811), *Pride and Prejudice* (1813), *Mansfield Park* (1814), and *Emma* (1816) — and her name appeared on none of them. *Northanger Abbey* and *Persuasion* were published posthumously in 1818. *Pride and Prejudice*, completed in August 1797 when she was only 21, and before *Sense and Sensibility*, was offered to a publisher by Mr Austen on 1 November of that year, and promptly declined. *Lady Susan* was a short novel in letter form, written in 1803, with a cynical tone and predatory female main character. Austen never tried to get it published, and after this exercise in feminine sexual wiles and wickedness she turned to less controversial and more ladylike material. This was followed by the unfinished novel known as *The Watsons*; Austen did not give it a title.

When *Sense and Sensibility* was published in 1811 by Egerton it was on condition that she sustained any loss; it sold out in 20 months and made Austen £140. As a result Egerton bought *Pride and Prejudice* in 1812 and published it the following year. In November 1815 she was in London to see *Emma* through the printers and, now celebrated and admired by the Prince Regent, she dedicated this novel to him, at his request.

Austen wrote two sets of three novels, with ten years between the sets. The first group, including *Pride and Prejudice*, is distinctively eighteenth century and the second recognisably Romantic and therefore more modern in feeling.

Pride and Prejudice

This was Austen's personal favourite of her works, which she referred to as her 'darling child', and it is perhaps the most popular classic novel in the

Pause for ***Thought***

Austen described *Pride and Prejudice* as 'rather too light, and bright, and sparkling' in a letter to her sister Cassandra in 1813. Do you agree? In what ways if so? Austen went on to say 'it wants to be stretched out here and there with a long chapter of sense'. Do you find the novel lacking in sense?

English language. Austen said of its heroine: 'I must confess that I think [Elizabeth] as delightful a creature as ever appeared in print, and how I shall be able to tolerate those who do not like her at least I do not know' (letter to Cassandra, 29 Jan 1813). This, her first mature novel, is more lively and humorous than later works, primarily because of the personality of its main character, who is the viewpoint wherever possible. Sisters were important in her work, and having five at once in *Pride and Prejudice* gave her scope to explore this relationship. All Elizabeth's sisters are a threat to her future in one way or another, and although their errors of judgement or character defects are turned into comedy, potential tragedy hovers throughout. Austen's achievement in this novel was to combine wit, drama and the traditions of poetic satire with those of the sentimental novel. Like her other novels, it is also a type of *Bildungsroman*, in which maturity is arrived at only after a painfully humbling learning process. It was first published, as usual for the time, in three volumes.

Historical context

Pride and Prejudice is set in Austen's own historical period (Regency England) and, although there are no directly political references in the novel, an understanding of the social and cultural milieu that provides the background to the events of the plot is required. In addition, details of houses, forms of transport, and leisure activities play a significant role in creating environment and atmosphere, and often carry symbolism indicative of the character concerned; without an understanding of what was considered proper behaviour at the time one cannot share the creator's judgement of her characters.

The period in which Austen was writing marks the cusp between Classicism and Romanticism in literature and the arts, so that elements of both can be found in her work.

War and revolution

England and France were at war throughout the period of Austen's writing, and her most famous novels were written and published during a time when there was a real danger of the French invading the country. The Napoleonic War was the largest-scale war on the European continent undertaken by England since the fifteenth century, and there was a clear political dimension: monarchical England was fighting against a revolutionary France that had executed its king, Louis XVI, in 1793 and replaced him with a government led by Napoleon. There was widespread fear among the British upper classes of a similar popular uprising in

Britain. The American War of Independence also affected English political life: the loss of the American colonies was thought to be a great disaster. Critics of *Pride and Prejudice* have complained that one would not guess that these momentous events were taking place at the time from reading the novel; soldiers exist in it, but only as potential husbands.

Regency England

George III, the third of the Hanoverian (German) kings of England, ascended the throne in 1760. Although he lived until 1820 he suffered from intermittent mental illness, and on several occasions Parliament transferred the monarch's powers to his son, the future George IV, who acted as Prince Regent. From 1810 onwards the arrangement became permanent, and this period (which came to be known as the Regency) coincided with a major upsurge in cultural life.

The word 'Regency' came to be synonymous with elegance, refinement and style. 'Beau' Brummel (1778–1840), the arbiter of taste and fashion in London, Bath and Brighton, was at one time a personal friend and protégé of the Regent. Brummel established the mode of men wearing fitted, well-cut clothes adorned with an elaborately-knotted cravat, a style known as the time as 'dandyism', the prototype of the modern suit and tie. He took five hours to dress, and recommended that boots be polished with champagne.

Political parties

Although England was described as having a constitutional monarchy, the king was sovereign only in name, real political power residing with the elected Parliament. During the eighteenth century, two significant factions formed within Parliament, the Whigs and the Tories. They were originally divided more by social background than by policies; the Whigs were mostly urban merchants who believed in free trade and economic liberalism; the Tories tended to include the aristocracy, country landowners and the Church of England. Austen's father, being a minister with a country living, was inevitably a Tory supporter, and predictably the political leanings of his daughter's approved characters were Tory because of their belonging to the country gentry.

Social and cultural context

The social hierarchy in England had not much changed since feudal times. The professionals, mainly doctors and lawyers, were considered

upper middle class and were treated more kindly by the gentry than those whose money came from trade, since they were educated. There was a developing mutual hostility between town and country dwellers; the latter had traditionally enjoyed higher social status but increasingly could not compete with urban wealth, although they still retained land ownership. There was little love lost between the gentry and aristocracy, the latter being viewed by the former as proud, idle and undeserving; Lady Catherine in *Pride and Prejudice* is a haughty bully.

> There was little love lost between the gentry and aristocracy

The country gentry at this time were at the height of their influence and prestige; their ownership of land, and therefore effectively of the tenant farmers and agricultural labourers who went with it, gave unique autonomy to the English gentleman on his estate. However, they recognised that they were under threat from the rise of an increasingly prosperous urban middle class who made their money from manufacturing. This social trend, accelerated by the industrial revolution, is represented by the Gardiners in *Pride and Prejudice*; they live in Cheapside, an unfashionable area of London, and are heartily despised by the Bingleys. This is ironic given that the Bingley fortune has all been acquired through trade.

The truly worthy thing to be, in Austen's eyes, was a gentleman, hence Elizabeth's comment that she is a 'gentleman's daughter' even though her mother is not considered to be a gentlewoman (although Mrs Bennet's sister married an attorney, her brother went into trade). It is a radical and provocative statement for Elizabeth to claim social equality with Darcy, whose mother, Lady Catherine's sister, was also titled, and whose grandfather was an earl.

Manners and morals

As far as etiquette was concerned it was important to be seen to do the right thing; one would be gossiped about if one offended against traditional behaviour or broke the rules of the community.

There were strict rules about visiting, and leaving one's card, and it is with just such a conversation that the novel begins. There were many pitfalls in the visiting game: it was a matter of courtesy for the head of the household to 'wait upon' a male newcomer to a neighbourhood, but it was a slight to visit before being visited, depending on the respective positions of those involved, or not to visit soon enough, or not to return a visit immediately (and Jane is only finally convinced of Caroline Bingley's treachery when she is faulted in this matter). Furthermore, having 'called', one had to stay the right amount of time, which was 15 minutes when calling on an acquaintance unannounced and uninvited. The caller had to leave a card if the 'callee' was not at home. One could not approach someone without being introduced, or introduce someone else if one had not been previously and formally introduced oneself (making it a social faux pas by Mr Collins to introduce himself to Darcy in Chapter 18).

The shame of social stigma

While Elizabeth suffers a degree of remorse for having been instrumental in allowing Lydia to run the risk of social stigma, she is also clear that Lydia's behaviour is unacceptable simply because of the shame it brings on the family. This condemnation is shared by the author, who does not question the idea that living with a man out of wedlock ruins a girl. Elizabeth, the voice of reason and common sense at this point in the novel, condemns Lydia's behaviour as 'infamy' and declares that if Lydia does not marry Wickham 'she is lost forever'. The only voice of moral relativism belongs to Mrs Bennet, who is so happy to have Lydia married that she does not care about the manner of its accomplishment, whereas even Mr Bennet manages to condemn both his youngest daughter and Wickham, saying: 'I will not encourage the impudence of either, by receiving them at Longbourn.'

Marriage

Families with no sons, as is the case in the Bennet family, were to be pitied as property could not pass down to any of the girls but could be 'entailed' to the nearest male relative, in this case the Reverend Mr Collins, a distant cousin of Mr Bennet, who will inherit the family home of Longbourn on the latter's death. Only elder sons could inherit their father's estate. Respectable occupations had to be found for younger sons: the second estate was the church, and the third was either the army or the navy.

It was an acquisitive society based on money and property, both of which could best be secured through inheritance and marriage. The status of an heiress, or the possession of a dowry or allowance, was a prerequisite for women to be considered attractive marriage prospects. On the other hand, women were potentially more socially mobile than men. Provided they were gentlewomen, of sound reputation and pretty, they could raise their social status through a good marriage, as Elizabeth and Jane do.

It was an acquisitive society based on money and property

The onus was on men to find someone rich to marry if they had no money themselves. To succeed in this objective a young man had to depend on charm or seduction; this could put young women's reputations in danger (as Wickham does three times — four including his flirtation with Elizabeth).

A woman's reputation (a euphemism for virtue or chastity) was vitally important to her whole family's social position as well as to her chances of attracting a suitor. When 'of age', which was 16, young females were paraded at balls to declare that they were 'out', so that eligible males could make their move. They were chaperoned by older married women, usually relatives, on the rare occasions they were allowed out in public. Except when dancing, it was almost impossible for single girls to have private conversations with men they were not at least engaged to, hence the excitement when a ball is announced, and the pressure Lydia puts upon Bingley to arrange one.

Marriage was assumed to be the social and biological destiny for all women of all classes in the eighteenth and nineteenth centuries. Austen explains the situation with reference to Charlotte Lucas:

> **Without thinking highly either of men or of matrimony, marriage had always been her object; it was the only honourable provision for well-educated young women of small fortune, and however uncertain of giving happiness, must be their pleasantest preservative from want (p. 120).**

This makes it clear how brave Elizabeth is being in turning down Mr Collins, for she cannot afford to be choosy. Austen herself turned down an offer she thought better of overnight, and became Aunt Jane as a result. Mary, being both plain and not at all accomplished, can expect to end up looking after her parents, pitied by society for being a spinster.

Marriage involved the wider family and not just the couple; Miss Bingley threatens Darcy with a 'charming mother-in-law' in the person of Mrs Bennet, and when Charlotte wins Mr Collins the whole family celebrates. The leading families looked to ally themselves with others of a similar rank, and often achieved this by the marriage of cousins so that the wealth and property could be kept in the family; this was Lady Catherine's plan for her daughter Anne and Darcy. Though wives were not independent in any sense, moving to their husband's establishment was the only possible freedom girls could aim for, and it was therefore as devoutly wished for by them as by their parents, who would otherwise have to continue to support them.

Marriage was possible at 16; by 18 it was positively desirable, and by 20 the worries of being left on the shelf as an old maid began, hence Charlotte's determination to catch Mr Collins (she is 27) and his warning to Elizabeth (who is already 21).

The army's eligible bachelors

The army, often known as 'redcoats' in literature as this made them more glamorous and dramatic, was composed of county regiments. Each regiment had a home barracks but some were posted to small towns on recruiting drives. Soldiers' pay was barely sufficient but their social status was quite high because the younger officers were eligible bachelors and therefore invited by the local gentry to all the events in the vicinity.

Gretna Green

The significance of the hope that Lydia and Wickham have eloped to the Scottish village of Gretna Green is that couples from England who wanted instant marriage with no questions asked went there. It was the nearest village over the Scottish border from England; Scottish marriage laws during the period 1754–1856 were much laxer than those in England, where marriage required a three-week period of residence and parental consent for those under 21. If Lydia and Wickham had gone to Gretna Green it was likely that they intended to marry rather than live in sin in London.

Evangelicalism and the Church of England

At the time Austen was writing, the established position of the Church of England had been threatened by a lively new religious movement, Evangelicalism, originating in the rapidly expanding industrial towns. Austen came to support this movement because it included a goal to reform morals and manners. She also became increasingly aware of and distressed by the apparent corruption and worldliness of the Church of England, as can be seen in her anti-clerical characterisation of Mr Collins, a self-aggrandising and self-promoting smug social climber with no genuine interest in serving his parishioners or setting a good moral example. Clergymen were not required to have a vocational calling, and appointment to a parish was often in the gift of the local lord of the manor, offering a means of subsistence with few duties involved. Wickham toyed with the idea of taking up the Pemberley living.

Titles of address

In Austen's work titles of address are an important mechanism for observing protocol and preserving propriety. As it was expected that girls in a family would marry in order of age, there was a convention that the eldest unmarried daughter in a family was called 'Miss' plus surname, hence Jane being referred to outside the family as 'Miss Bennet' and the other sisters by just their first name (even by the author: 'Elizabeth was disgusted, and even Miss Bennet was shocked').

When socialising outside the family, where first names are not appropriate, the younger daughters are called by their full name, e.g. Miss Elizabeth Bennet (whereas Jane is never 'Miss Jane Bennet').

…titles of address are an important mechanism for observing protocol and preserving propriety

Married woman immediately became known by their married title and husband's surname, and lost their first name, like Mrs Hurst. For girls to become 'Mrs' was a rite of passage much longed for, as in Lydia's case, since married women took precedence over older unmarried ones (as Lydia is quick to remind Jane when she visits home as Mrs Wickham).

Men were always referred to as 'Mr', hence the anomaly of the main characters in *Pride and Prejudice* being known as Elizabeth and Mr Darcy, not an equal partnership. (Many readers would not readily recall Bingley's, or even Darcy's, first names, so little are they used in the novel.) If the 'Mr' were dropped (and this was often considered impolite), men were referred to by their surname not their Christian name. Even close friends observed distinctions of rank and did not use first names even in private, especially to a social superior.

Family relationships required formal titles, so for instance Mrs Bennet refers to 'my sister Philips' and Elizabeth's letter from her aunt is signed 'M. Gardiner'. Married couples, even when alone, referred to each other as Mr and Mrs plus their surname, as the Bennets do (and in fact they are not even given first names). Servants were usually called by their surname only, whether male or female.

Family life

The number of domestic servants was an indicator of status, and servants had a hierarchy of their own, from housekeeper down to scullery maid, with the lady's maid in a special category of her own as an intimate companion of the lady of the house.

The bond between children and parents was not always strong at that time; the children of gentry were brought up by nurses and governesses and the father was often a physically or mentally distant figure. As a result, siblings often became very close, especially the girls, who had to stay at home so much.

Effective contraception was not available (the only method was a condom made of animal gut), and often not practised at all. The risk of an unmarried pregnancy, to which Lydia assuredly exposed herself by her actions, would have brought the greatest shame to the family. It was not unusual for a woman to be permanently pregnant. The infant mortality rate was very high: 20% of babies died in their first year, and one in three children before their sixth birthday (the life expectancy was only 35 at the turn of the century), so that despite the number of children born, a large family was quite unusual. The aim of parents was to have sons (at least two, 'an heir and a spare'), so five daughters were considered a disaster, as each needed to be provided with a dowry or allowance to attract a husband.

Country life

Lords of the manor, apart from engaging in hunting, shooting and fishing, did very little as they had a large staff to see to the running of the house, garden and estate. It was not uncommon for large country properties to be rented out for a period of several months, as Netherfield Hall is, to town folk wanting to entertain grandly and to enjoy rural pursuits. The higher gentry usually had a house in London, as Darcy does, in addition to their country estate, so that they could be in town for the social season.

Travel was by horse-drawn carriage or on horseback, and slow. It takes Elizabeth an overnight stop and half of the next day to get home in a coach from Derbyshire to Hertfordshire, arriving 'by dinner-time' the day after she sets off. Being cut off from neighbours and towns, and with few diversions, country house owners encouraged visitors.

The lady of the house, not having even sport as a hobby and largely confined to the house, passed her time when at home in embroidering, sketching, and piano-playing. Dancing was much prized by the young as a rare opportunity for men and women to converse privately and have some physical contact; it was condoned by parents as allowing legitimate proximity but not licentiousness. Unlike the sons, who were sent away to public schools at the age of seven, daughters would be tutored at home, usually by a governess. Lady Catherine is shocked that the Bennet girls did not have a governess (but nor did Austen). Girls were in general not expected to become proficient at anything more than domestic accomplishments and basic literacy and numeracy.

Costume

What men and women wore had an effect, then as now, on the options and limitations of their behaviour. Full-length flimsy dresses — whose role was primarily decorative and intended for the drawing room — and elaborate hair styles restricted women's physical movements indoors and their ability to do much outdoors, such as go for vigorous country rambles, be out in inclement weather or ride horses seriously. They had no pockets or any way of secreting things about their person except into the cleavage of their empire-line frocks, which exposed the neck and made young ladies vulnerable to chills. Raincoats did not exist, nor cold-weather gear, and hats, gloves and footwear were decorative rather than functional.

> What men and women wore had an effect...on their behaviour

Film and television productions cannot always be relied upon to give an accurate impression of the clothing of the period. Try to find some contemporary illustrations of the clothing worn by the kind of people Austen writes about.

Women possessed a limited number of 'gowns', as they were relatively expensive and had to be made to order by a seamstress, after material had been purchased from a local haberdasher who often had to bring it from London. What to wear was therefore not only an important but also a time-consuming matter, hence the flutter caused by an upcoming ball or any social engagement. The type and quality of the fabric used for gowns was an indication of social status. Re-trimming an old bonnet was often the only way of pretending to have a new one. Hair was long, which required a maid to brush it in the evening, put it in papers overnight, and pin it up in the morning, often with the use of curling tongs, heated in the fire, for the fringe and side pieces.

The *beau monde*

The London Season was a relatively short period of time beginning shortly after Easter, when Parliament was recalled, and ending on 12 August, when Parliament went into recess and the grouse-shooting season opened. Once the Season was over, members of society went either to their country houses or to seaside spas; the latter gave people of all ages a chance to enjoy fresh air, good company and good food. Visits to such resorts were essential for socially active and ambitious people, as these watering places were the hub of social life in the summer. At places such as Brighton, Weymouth and the inland spa at Bath, balls and assemblies took place every night, while the days were filled with the social activities unique to resort life: garden, water, card and dancing parties. In Bath, attendance at the pump rooms provided an excuse for finding husbands; under the guise of seeking the curative spa waters matrons could dispose of their daughters. Here, although still regulated by the conventions of Regency propriety, couples had opportunities to meet and get to know one another.

Literary context

Critical history

Pride and Prejudice remains one of the most widely read novels in English and in 2005 was voted the most romantic novel of all time. In the mid-nineteenth century, however, the best-known female writers, Charlotte Brontë, Elizabeth Barrett Browning and George Eliot, were all unimpressed by Austen's work, which they described as limited.

From the 1870s onwards, as a result of the publication by her nephew, James Edward Austen-Leigh, of his *A Memoir of Jane Austen* (1870), public interest in Austen grew and she became more widely known, especially in America. Austen-Leigh praised her gift of the 'intuitive perception of genius', but also created a bland legend around her, which probably did her a disservice: 'of events her life was singularly barren: few changes and no great crises ever broke the smooth current of its course [...] There was in her nothing eccentric or angular; no ruggedness of temper; no singularity of manner...'

A. C. Bradley's essay of 1911 was the first to draw attention to her ties to Dr Johnson, to her being a moralist as well as a humorist, and to her use of the ironic authorial viewpoint, which allows us to realise how different things are from the way the characters see them. Over the next few years, appreciation for her subtlety gained ground.

In 1940 an essay by the academic psychologist D. W. Harding, 'Regular hatred: an aspect of the work of Jane Austen', was published. He attacks the established notion that she was a kindly writer by analysing her use of satire, asserting that she was an intelligent and sensitive woman who found it almost intolerable to live among people less acute of mind and feeling than herself. In fact, he says, she hated such people, but since society would not allow her to express her hatred directly, she wrote novels as an outlet through which she could articulate her contempt for her inferiors and for the society that protected them. It signalled a move towards a Freudian viewpoint, drawing attention to the Electra complex whereby the heroine hates her mother, loves her father, rejects a suitor who is the opposite of her father and accepts a lover who can be a father-substitute.

Austen scholarship became more divided in the latter part of the twentieth century, when, fuelled by a wave of new film adaptations, popular interest in her work exploded. Marxists either rejected her for being bourgeois or tried to claim her as a pre-Marxian Marxist (as feminists have tried to claim her as a pre-feminist feminist) who exposes the economic basis of social behaviour.

Austen: a 'feminist' writer?

The rise of women writers — though there were only a handful of them — coincided with the rise of the novel, which was, thanks to eighteenth-century circulating libraries, catering for bored and closeted females interested in the escapist fantasy literature of romance and Gothic horror. Early female novelists often used their writing to gain the attention and

The rise of women writers... coincided with the rise of the novel

approval of their fathers, as Austen herself did, and Elizabeth Bennet seems to wish to please her father by her use of words and wit.

Austen felt compelled by social disapproval of women writers to describe herself merely, but categorically, as 'A Lady' on the title page of her first published novel; this need to conceal female identity continued throughout the nineteenth century, with the adoption of male pseudonyms by the Brontë sisters (Acton, Ellis and Currer Bell) and by Mary Ann Evans (George Eliot). Early female writers found it incompatible to be wives and mothers as well as writers, and generally did not attempt both, though Mary Wollstonecraft was a notable exception. Men, whether writers or not, usually had a study or library to retreat to (as illustrated by Mr Bennet); Austen had to write covertly in the parlour.

Though the word and concept of feminism did not exist, some writers are before their time; the argument for Austen as a proto-feminist rests on how unconventional Elizabeth Bennet and her other heroines can be proved to be, on the degree of their independence of mind and on their role as a catalyst for change. Those who do not accept that Austen was a feminist cite the marriages with which the novel ends, which they see as confirming the patriarchal traditions and social expectations of a woman gratefully agreeing to settle down with an older, richer and more experienced man, and thereby entering into an unequal partnership. Elizabeth, as mistress of Pemberley, could have continued to be a thorn in the flesh of the nobility and establishment with her cutting observations, but the novel specifically tells us that she has learned to suppress her critical and teasing tendencies, and has even accepted the presence of Lady Catherine de Bourgh in her house. Although Mr Collins is mocked for his view that rank inevitably excites 'silence and respect' (p. 104), it could be argued that these are exactly the qualities that Elizabeth is forced to embrace as the price of her alliance with the Darcy clan. However reluctant Austen may have been to gag her heroine, the social reality was that women had to learn to be subservient.

The alternative viewpoint, that Austen was indeed a feminist, is put by S. Gilbert and S. Gubar in *The Madwoman in the Attic* (1979), their seminal work on the woman writer and the nineteenth-century imagination. Vivien Jones (introduction to Penguin Classics edition) also claims feminist credentials for Austen's heroine: 'Elizabeth Bennet seems to connect most directly with the active, visible, independent identity of modern femininity', and she sees her as stronger than Darcy in that 'his social and moral confidence are challenged by her uncompromising criticism'.

It has been argued that Austen is being subversive in that, while simultaneously appearing to punish assertive female behaviour and to recommend restraint and docility, she duplicitously reveals the delights of non-conformity and rewards her heroines for their rebellious traits; this comes through strongly in both the Collins and Lady Catherine put-down scenes, and in Elizabeth being awarded the ultimate prize of Darcy. In addition many critics, not all feminists, have noted the lack of conviction of her endings, the way couples are brought with indecent authorial haste (and apparent authorial indifference) to the altar and the brink of a supposed wedded bliss.

Gilbert and Gubar also argue that though she is a supremely unattractive character Lady Catherine has independence and bows to no expectations but her own; she is a powerful and furious female who 'sees no occasion for entailing estates from the female lines' (p. 161) and is therefore opposed to the very basis of patriarchy, which is the exclusive right of male inheritance. She is vilified as a representative of matriarchal power because she is patronising, egotistical and rude, but it is possible to see her as a proto-feminist who is surprisingly similar to Elizabeth in being forthright, authoritative and strong-willed. 'You give your opinion very decidedly for so young a person' (p. 162) could be a compliment rather than a criticism. When Elizabeth marries Darcy she takes the intended place of Lady Catherine's daughter, one much more in her own image than her real daughter, and it is thanks to her ladyship that the couple are brought together.

Vivien Jones argues that Elizabeth is a post-feminist rather than a pre-feminist heroine, who supports what is valuable from both the traditional and radical standpoints and is thus a force for change as well as reconciliation and consolidation. She claims that a resolution is achieved whereby the old and new are synthesised in the union of the mercantile money of the enterprising class of the Gardiners with the old money and property of the ruling elite of the Darcy family. This union brings revolutionary tendencies into the fold where they can do no damage and where they can provide vitality and reinvigoration. This is prefigured by the fact that Darcy and Mr Gardiner combine forces to save Lydia's name and the Bennet family's position in society.

TASK 21

Do you think there is any evidence that Austen was in any sense a 'feminist' writer, or is this a retrospective imposition of a twentieth-century concept?

Working with the text

Meeting the Assessment Objectives

The four key English Literature Assessment Objectives (AOs) describe the different skills you need to show in order to get a good grade. Regardless of what texts or which examination specification you are following, these AOs lie at the heart of your study of English literature at AS and A2; they let you know exactly what the examiners are looking for and provide a helpful framework for your literary studies.

The Assessment Objectives require you to:

- articulate creative, informed and relevant responses to literary texts, using appropriate terminology and concepts, and coherent, accurate written expression **(AO1)**
- demonstrate detailed critical understanding in analysing the ways in which structure, form and language shape meanings in literary texts **(AO2)**
- explore connections and comparisons between different literary texts, informed by interpretations of other readers **(AO3)**
- demonstrate understanding of the significance and influence of the contexts in which literary texts are written and understood **(AO4)**

Try to bear in mind that the AOs are there to support rather than restrict you; do not look at them as encouraging a tick-box approach or a mechanistic reductive way into the study of literature. Examination questions are written with the AOs in mind, so if you answer them clearly and carefully you should automatically hit the right targets. If you are devising your own questions for coursework, seek the help of your teacher to ensure that your essay title is carefully worded to liberate the required assessment objectives so that you can do your best.

Although the Assessment Objectives are common to all the exam boards, specifications vary enormously in the way they meet the requirements.

The boards' websites provide useful information, including sections for students, past papers, sample papers and mark schemes.

AQA: www.aqa.org.uk

EDEXCEL : www.edexcel.com

OCR: www.ocr.org.uk

WJEC: www.wjec.co.uk

Remember, though, that your knowledge and understanding of the text still lie at the heart of A-level study, as they always have done. While what constitutes a text may vary according to the specification you are following (e.g. it could be an article, extract, letter, diary, critical essay, review, novel, play or poem), and there may be an emphasis on the different ways in which texts can be interpreted and considered in relation to different contexts, in the end the study of literature starts with, and comes back to, your engagement with the text itself.

Working with AO1

AO1 focuses upon literary and critical insight, organisation of material and clarity of written communication. Examiners are looking for accurate spelling and grammar and clarity of thought and expression, so say what you want to say, and say it as clearly as you can.

Aim for cohesion; your ideas should be presented coherently with an overall sense of a developing argument. Think carefully about your introduction, because your opening paragraph not only sets the agenda for your response but provides the reader with a strong first impression of you — positive or negative.

Try to use 'appropriate terminology' but do not hide behind fancy critical terms or complicated language you do not fully understand; 'feature-spotting' and merely listing literary terms is a classic banana skin all examiners are familiar with.

Choose your references carefully; copying out great gobbets of a text learned by heart underlines your inability to select the choicest short quotation with which to clinch your argument. Regurgitating chunks of material printed on the examination paper without detailed critical analysis is — for obvious reasons — a reductive exercise; instead try to incorporate brief quotations into your own sentences, weaving them in seamlessly to illustrate your points and develop your argument.

The hallmarks of a well-written essay — whether for coursework or in an exam — include a clear, coherent introduction that orientates

the reader, a systematic and logical argument, aptly chosen and neatly embedded quotations and a conclusion which consolidates your case.

Working with AO2

In studying a text you should think about its overall form (novel, sonnet, tragedy, farce etc.), structure (how it is organised, how its constituent parts connect with each other) and language.

In studying a long novel or a play it might be better to begin with the larger elements of form and structure before considering language, whereas analysing aspects of a poem's language (imagery, for example) might be a more appropriate place to start. If 'form is meaning', what are the implications of your chosen writer's decision to select this specific genre? In terms of structure, why does the on-stage action of one play unfold in real time while another spans months or years? In terms of language features, what is most striking about the diction of your text — dialogue, dialect, imagery or symbolism?

In order to discuss language in detail you will need to quote from the text — but the mere act of quoting is not enough to meet AO2. What is important is what you do with the quotation — how you analyse it and how it illuminates your argument. Moreover, since you will often need to make points about larger generic and organisational features of your chosen text, such as books, chapters, verses, cantos, acts or scenes which are usually much too long to quote, being able to reference effectively is just as important as mastering the art of the embedded quotation.

Working with AO3

AO3 is a double Assessment Objective which asks you to 'explore connections and comparisons' between texts as well as showing your understanding of the views and interpretations of others. You will find it easier to make comparisons and connections between texts (of any kind) if you try to balance them as you write; remember also that connections and comparisons are not only about finding similarities — differences are just as interesting. Above all, consider how the comparison illuminates each text. It's not just a matter of finding the relationships and connections but of analysing what they show. When writing comparatively use words and constructions that will help you to link your texts, such as whereas, on the other hand, while, in contrast, by comparison, as in, differently, similarly, comparably.

To access the second half of AO3 effectively you need to measure your own interpretation of a text against those of your teacher and other students. By all means refer to named critics and quote from them if it seems appropriate, but the examiners are most interested in your personal and creative response. If your teacher takes a particular critical line, be prepared to challenge and question it; there is nothing more dispiriting for an examiner than to read a set of scripts from one centre which all say exactly the same thing. Top candidates produce fresh personal responses rather than merely regurgitating the ideas of others, however famous or insightful their interpretations may be.

Of course your interpretation will only be convincing if it is supported by clear reference to the text, and you will only be able to evaluate other readers' ideas if you test them against the evidence of the text itself. Worthwhile AO3 means more than quoting someone else's point of view and saying you agree, although it can be very helpful to use critical views if they push forward an argument of your own and you can offer relevant textual support. Look for other ways of reading texts — from a Marxist, feminist, new historicist, post-structuralist, psychoanalytic, dominant or oppositional point of view — which are more creative and original than merely copying out the ideas of just one person.

Try to show an awareness of multiple readings with regard to your chosen text and an understanding that the meaning of a text is dependent as much upon what the reader brings to it as what the writer left there. Using modal verb phrases such as 'may be seen as', 'might be interpreted as' or 'could be represented as' implies that you are aware that different readers interpret texts in different ways at different times. The key word here is plurality; there is no single meaning, no right answer, and you need to evaluate a range of other ways of making textual meanings as you work towards your own.

Working with AO4

AO4, with its emphasis on the 'significance and influence' of the 'contexts in which literary texts are written and received', might at first seem less deeply rooted in the text itself but in fact you are considering and evaluating here the relationship between the text and its contexts. Note the word 'received': this refers to the way interpretation can be influenced by the specific contexts within which the reader is operating. When you are studying a text written many years ago, there is often an immense gulf between its original contemporary context of production and the twenty-first century context in which you receive it.

To access AO4 successfully you need to think about how contexts of production, reception, literature, culture, biography, geography, society,

history, genre and intertextuality can affect texts. Place the text at the heart of the web of contextual factors which you feel have had the most impact upon it; examiners want to see a sense of contextual alertness woven seamlessly into the fabric of your essay rather than a clumsy bolted-on rehash of a website or your old history notes. Try to convey your awareness of the fact that literary works contain embedded and encoded representations of the cultural, moral, religious, racial and political values of the society from which they emerged, and that over time attitudes and ideas change until the views they reflect are no longer widely shared. And you're right to think that there must be an overlap between a focus on interpretations (AO3) and a focus on contexts, so do not worry about pigeonholing the AOs here.

Extended commentary

This is an example of a commentary on two extracts from the novel — Lydia's letter in Chapter 47 (p. 276–77) and part of Darcy's letter to Elizabeth in Chapter 35 (pp. 191–94) — with a view to the requirements of AO2.

Lydia's and Darcy's letters compared

In Austen there is an expectation that characters produce their very best English when writing letters, especially to people who are only acquaintances and not family, as this is a permanent form and one by which other characters, as well as the reader, have an opportunity to judge the quality of their expression. Lydia writes as she speaks, thoughtlessly and chaotically, but her writing is a greater indictment of her than is her verbal expression when she chats to her sisters. In context, Lydia's letter should be at best contrite and at least informative and serious, but the aim is clearly to exult and show off.

The verb 'laugh' used immediately is associated throughout the novel with Lydia. It is a fault in her character and behaviour that she should find serious topics amusing and give way to unladylike expression of her thoughts and reference to physical actions. The letter favours coordination rather than subordination in its sentence structures. This is in contrast to Austen's morally approved of and better educated characters. The use of 'with who' in the second sentence is ungrammatical. This steers the reader into believing that Lydia is either ignorant or uncaring of correct expression, and, because an abuser of language, likely to have deficiencies in other aspects of her life. She calls her correspondent Harriet Forster (the wife of Colonel Forster, Commanding Officer of Wickham's regiment, and considerably older than herself) a 'simpleton', which is too casual and insulting a word to be applied to someone senior and to whom she owes gratitude for having invited her to Brighton. To call Wickham 'an angel' is risibly inappropriate and stresses her lack of judgement and her view of life as a romantic delusion. She generally employs extremes and superlatives, which means that she is excessive in deed as well as word. Romantic clichés pepper her letter, as in 'I should never be happy without him', which do not sit well with such vulgar phrases as 'think it no harm to be off.' Many of the words Lydia uses are monosyllabic and do not live up to the standard of elegant utterance expected of polite society.

That she values surprising her parents over her filial duty towards them would have been seen as shocking at the time. With Lydia, drama and jokes are everything, thus showing the triviality of her mind. The exclamation mark, much favoured in all her utterances, is represented here also. How very inappropriate to be referring to another beau, the unfortunately named 'Pratt', when she has chosen her future partner already, and it is also not becoming that she should expect Harriet to pass on messages to soldiers for her. Reference to servants is not considered to be *à propos* in Austen's novels, and it is especially odd to find 'Sally' being named in a letter of such significance, implying that Lydia is incapable of understanding the effect that her elopement is going to have on others, and that she would not care if she did. It is more important to her to change her name and take precedence over her four elder sisters by being the first to be married. It is symbolic that there is 'a great slit' in her muslin gown, but her reputation will not be mended as easily. She ends her letter as vulgarly as she began, giving inappropriate 'love' to Colonel Forster and mentioning alcohol. The letter has neither a proper opening nor conclusion, showing a lack of consideration of content and of formal letter-writing etiquette.

Throughout the novel the way characters select topics, choose vocabulary and form syntax is indicative of their moral standing, and here we see Lydia failing in all three areas by treating the serious matter of her elopement as being of no more consequence than her clothing, by using repetitive and common or immoderate language, and by being unable to write in paragraphs.

A comparison with the structure and language of Darcy's letter in Chapter 35 shows how much is deficient in Lydia's letter. Darcy's tone is the opposite of exuberant, and this is not only because of the seriousness and delicacy of the content, but because every word has been carefully chosen to be decorous, elegant, and eloquent. He never uses a monosyllabic word when there is a longer synonym, and abstract nouns are the keynote of the letter, as they are of Austen's own narrative language and of all her heroes and heroines. Where Lydia would use

the word 'try', Darcy uses 'endeavour'; where she uses 'love' he uses 'sentiment'. Each sentence links to the previous one in developing its ideas, so that the letter has not only an overall structure but internal sequencing and cohesion. The sentences are complex, indicating that an intelligent mind is at work, one seeking to establish causes and effects in a logical manner. Each sentence has several clauses, some embedded, with many commas, which show control of syntax and competence in being able to express himself precisely and concisely. Words like 'apprehension', 'repugnance', 'impartial', 'propriety' and 'esteemed' are not only beyond Lydia's vocabulary, they are beyond her cognition. 'But I shall not scruple to assert' is a construction and use of vocabulary which places Darcy as an aristocrat in the use of language. Many of the sentences are finely balanced around an antithesis or consist of a tripartite structure in the rhetorical mode of the Augustan essayists, such as Dr Johnson, admired by Austen: for example, 'If *you* have not been mistaken here, *I* must have been in an error' (p. 192), or 'The situation of your mother's family, though objectionable, was nothing in comparison of that total want of propriety so frequently, so almost uniformly betrayed by herself, by your three younger sisters, and occasionally even by your father' (p. 193).

Perhaps there is something too formal, too stilted and inflexible in the structure and language, since it is Austen's method to allow language to reveal personality and Darcy has yet to learn to become more yielding. Concern, consideration and intelligence are present in the style, however, and ease can come later. The opposite is harder to achieve, and there is no evidence in Lydia's letter that she can become a respecter of words and therefore of morals and of people. In Austen's use of direct speech — which is what a letter is, in written form — structure and language shape character and the reader's understanding of it.

Essay planning

See the free website at **www.philipallan.co.uk/literatureguidesonline** for sample essays, with grades and examiner's comments, and for further questions. Answers to the questions set as tasks in this section are also given online.

Comparative essay: whole-novel question

Examples of works with which *Pride and Prejudice* may be compared are *The French Lieutenant's Woman* by John Fowles or *The Yellow Wallpaper* by Charlotte Perkins Gilman. In both of these works the relationships of power and independence between women and men are explored. Both may be seen as feminist works — a fruitful avenue of comparison with *Pride and Prejudice*. In terms of form, structure and language, *The French Lieutenant's Woman* is a post-modern novel for which Fowles offers three alternative endings. *The Yellow Wallpaper* is told as a series of short 'journal entries' made by the woman in a secret journal.

Sample question

'*Pride and Prejudice* is preoccupied with surfaces and never gets beneath them.' Explore the ways in which writers present the worlds of their novels.

In your response, you should focus on *Pride and Prejudice* to establish your argument and you should refer to the second text you have read to support and develop your line of argument.

Indicative content

Responses may include reference to:

- the various surfaces presented: the physical surfaces — Longbourn, Netherfield, Pemberley; the social surfaces presented by Darcy, Wickham, Elizabeth, Jane, Mr. Collins, Lady Catherine
- the roles of these surfaces in developing other aspects of the narrative such as irony and theme
- the proposition — to what extent the surfaces are a preoccupation and how far Austen gets beneath them
- the methods used to present and develop the theme, such as imagery, dialogue, diction, setting and characterisation

The text used to develop the line of argument may show contrasting or similar uses of surfaces.

In order to meet the AO2 requirement, there should be specific comment on technique and method in the presentation of 'the worlds of the novels' — the terms of the question lead to this.

Top band descriptors

- Responds with a sustained argument in an informed and relevant manner
- Makes sustained and pertinent use of literary terms and concepts to develop a coherent argument
- Displays accurate and fluent written expression
- Constructs an original and creative response in a well-developed argument

---

TASK *22*

Make notes for the possible content of an essay answering the following question:

'Female characters are often represented as being constrained by their societies.' Explore the presentation of female characters in the light of this statement.

In your response you should focus on *Pride and Prejudice* to establish your argument, and you should refer to the second text you have read to support and develop your line of argument.

Comparative essay: extract-based question

Sample question

'In *Pride and Prejudice* Jane Austen is essentially writing about self-knowledge.' Using *Pride and Prejudice* p. 200 as your starting point, from 'She perfectly remembered every thing that had passed in conversation between Wickham and herself,' to '"Till this moment, I never knew myself"' on p. 202, explore the methods writers use to develop the theme of self-knowledge.

In your response, you should focus on *Pride and Prejudice* to establish your argument and you should refer to the second text you have read to support and develop your line of argument.

Indicative content

Responses may include reference to:
- the particular passage and its role in developing the theme
- the growth of self-knowledge in characters besides Elizabeth (e.g. Darcy)
- the apparent lack of self-knowledge in some other characters (e.g. Lydia, Lady Catherine, the Bingley sisters) and Austen's presentation of change in this respect
- the importance of the theme in the overall context of the book
- representations of gender
- possible responses of readers to the growth (or lack of it) in the self-knowledge of the characters
- the methods used to present the theme, e.g. imagery, dialogue, characterisation, setting, diction.

The connections made between *Pride and Prejudice* and the text used to develop the line of argument are likely to explore the theme of self-knowledge, its importance and the ways in which it is presented. There may be some discussion of whether or not this is a central theme.

In order to meet the AO2 requirement, there should be specific comment on technique and method in the presentation of 'self-knowledge' — the terms of the question lead to this.

Top band descriptors
- Responds with a sustained argument in an informed and relevant manner
- Makes sustained and pertinent use of literary terms and concepts to develop a coherent argument
- Displays accurate and fluent written expression
- Constructs an original and creative response in a well-developed argument

---

TASK 23

Make notes for the possible content of an essay answering the following question:

'There is always a huge contrast between the behaviour of men and women.' Using *Pride and Prejudice*, Chapter 19, p. 104, as your starting point from '"You are too hasty, sir," she cried' to '"as would be consistent with the true delicacy of the female character"' at the bottom of p. 105, explore the presentation of the behaviour of men and women.

In your response you should focus on *Pride and Prejudice* to establish your argument, and you should refer to the second text you have read to support and develop your line of argument.

PHILIP ALLAN LITERATURE GUIDE **FOR A-LEVEL**

Whole-novel essay questions

Sample question 1

'In *Pride and Prejudice*, marriage is presented primarily as an economic arrangement.' How far and in what ways do you agree with this view?

Top band descriptors

- **AO1** Answers should be fluent and well constructed, showing a creative engagement with the text. Candidates should demonstrate detailed knowledge of marriages and attitudes to marriage in *Pride and Prejudice*, selecting telling illustrative material and using appropriate terminology with confidence.

- **AO2** Essays should analyse with confidence ways in which Austen presents marriage, considering the effectiveness of aspects such as narrative voice, dialogue, irony and structure.

- **AO3** Answers should offer a coherently argued view which is usefully informed by the interpretations of other readers. Candidates may make helpful comparisons with additional appropriate texts, e.g. other novels by Austen.

- **AO4** Answers should show informed insight into the importance of contextual issues such as the role of women and the nature of marriage in the society in which the novel is set.

Sample question 2

What importance does Mr Collins have in the whole of *Pride and Prejudice*?

Possible content

Comment might be made on Collins's comic role; on the way he reveals the characters of Mr Bennet, Elizabeth and Charlotte; on the way he is used to reveal attitudes to social class; as a negative representation of the church; as part of the love interest for Elizabeth as a foil to Darcy; as showing that Austen's heroine will only marry for love; as a contrast to Darcy; as a vehicle for irony; to reveal different attitudes to marriage; as a plot device to bring Darcy and Elizabeth together at Hunsford etc.

> **TASK 24**
>
> Make a plan for an essay answering the following question:
>
> **Examine the novel's presentation of the distinctions and relations between different social groups.**

Extract-based whole-novel discussion

Sample question

(a) How does Austen tell the story in Chapter 16?

(b) Some readers see Wickham simply as a villain. How do you respond to his character and role in *Pride and Prejudice* as a whole?

Top band descriptors and indicative content

Part (a) AO2 descriptors:

- exploration and analysis of key aspects of form, with perceptive evaluation of how they shape meanings
- exploration and analysis of key aspects of structure, with perceptive evaluation of how they shape meanings;
- exploration and analysis of key aspects of language, with perceptive evaluation of how they shape meanings

Part (b) AOs 1, 3 and 4 descriptors:

- **AO1** Use of appropriate critical vocabulary and technically fluent expression/always relevant with very sharp focus on task
- **AO3** Perceptive consideration of some different interpretations of texts with sharp evaluation of their strengths and weaknesses
- **AO4** Excellent understanding of a range of contextual factors with specific, detailed links between context/texts/task

Indicative content for Part (a):

- Narrative perspective/voices: omniscient narrator, use of authorial commentary, use of voices, comic tone, etc.
- Setting: Mrs Philips's house, one evening, etc.
- Social comedy; romance, etc.
- Linear chronology: direct opening of how the Bennet sisters, Mr Collins and Mr Wickham are to attend the party at Mr and Mrs Philips's; dramatic centre – Elizabeth's conversation with Wickham about his past with Darcy; importance of Wickham's lie to the overall structure of the novel; comic ending with the focus on Lydia's stupidity and Collins's lack of social graces, etc.
- Formal, Latinate diction; use of irony; use of dialogue; use of contrast; use of comedy; verbs of saying, etc.

Indicative content for Part (b):

- Wickham's role as a villain in lying to Elizabeth, in causing ill feeling, in his desire for revenge on Darcy, in attempting to elope with Georgiana, in his seduction and running away with Lydia, etc.
- Wickham's role in being an obstacle in the relationship between Darcy and Elizabeth
- Wickham's contribution to the themes of money, marriage and prejudice and the changing values of society
- Wickham's sexual charm and dynamic energy
- Wickham's contribution to the morality of the novel since he gets his just deserts in the novel's conclusion, etc.

TASK 25

Make notes for the possible content of an essay answering the following two-part question:

(a) How does Austen tell the story in Chapter 35?

(b) What uses does Austen make of letters in *Pride and Prejudice* as a whole?

Top ten quotations

She was a woman of mean understanding, little information, and uncertain temper. (p. 7, about Mrs Bennet)

The triple structure in this descriptive sentence is typical of Austen's authorial style, and that favoured by her eighteenth-century models. Her dismissive criticism of Elizabeth's mother is unusually harsh, and reveals the author's priorities when judging character. It is not surprising that at least two of her daughters are wayward, and that Elizabeth, her father, and Darcy, all find her silly and embarrassing. One might argue that she cannot help being stupid, and that this makes her less culpable than someone more intelligent and better educated who should know better, such as her husband or Mr Collins.

'There is a mixture of servility and self-importance in his letter, which promises well.' (p. 63, Mr Bennet to Elizabeth about Mr Collins)

The paradox which is Mr Collins, both obsequious and pompous, is summed up by the perceptive Mr Bennet. Instead, however, of being alarmed by his cousin's impending visit and his entitlement to Longbourn, Mr Bennet looks forward to being entertained by him, showing how unsuitable he is as the head of his family.

'There is a stubbornness about me that never can bear to be frightened at the will of others. My courage always rises with every attempt to intimidate me.' (p. 170, Elizabeth)

Elizabeth proves, by standing up to Darcy when she thinks he has misused Wickham, and to Lady Catherine when she tries to pressurise her, that she is not frightened of others, however socially elevated. Her insistence on going to Jane at Netherfield, in inclement weather and without transport, proves her stubbornness and disregard for social conventions. This makes her a rebel in the context, and by comparison with others such as Charlotte and Sir William Lucas.

'Could you expect me to rejoice in the inferiority of your connections? To congratulate myself on the hope of relations, whose condition in life is so decidedly beneath my own?' (p. 188, Darcy to Elizabeth)

As readers we do sympathise with Darcy's view, given the embarrassing public behaviour of Mrs Bennet and Lydia, but on the other hand we feel how offensive this utterance is to Elizabeth. The way Darcy expresses himself sounds pompous and arrogant, as well as insensitive

to Elizabeth's feelings. He will have to go some way to redeem himself, therefore, in her and our eyes.

5

'I had not known you a month before I felt that you were the last man in the world whom I could ever be prevailed on to marry.' (p. 188, Elizabeth to Darcy)

This absolute and extreme statement shows that she is not always rational in her reactions to others, and that, as in the novel's original title, she is prone to be influenced by first impressions. This is also an example of the use of naive narration, and of Austen's use of irony.

6

Of neither Darcy nor Wickham could she think, without feeling that she had been blind, partial, prejudiced, absurd. (p. 201, about Elizabeth)

Elizabeth's ability to judge herself, to identify her faults, to learn through error, is what makes her a heroine. We admire her for her willingness to self-evaluate and condemn herself for the weaknesses she inherited from her parents and has hitherto not had cause to question.

7

'...obstinacy is the real defect of his character after all. He has been accused of many faults at different times; but *this* is the true one.' (p. 306, Mrs Gardiner in a letter to Elizabeth about Darcy)

If obstinacy is his real fault, and Elizabeth's is stubbornness, then this makes them equal, and we can see these qualities as evidence of spirit and independence, and therefore more admirable than either pride or prejudice. Neither of them will abandon a principle or give way to others who attempt to influence or pressure them. The novel positions the reader to despise those characters who do, such as Mr Collins, Charlotte, Bingley and Mr Bennet.

8

'He is a gentleman; I am a gentleman's daughter; so far we are equal.' (p. 337, Elizabeth to Lady Catherine)

For Elizabeth, and Austen, this is a very important claim. As a clergyman's daughter, Austen knew that she was a gentleman's daughter but was well aware that her family was not accepted as equals by the local gentry. The range of the social category 'gentleman' is shown by the fact that Elizabeth can claim equality with Darcy, who is related to aristocracy. As well as drawing attention to class labelling — and the dominance of the father over the mother in determining this — her utterance shows her spirited and loyal defence of her family in the face of the attempted bullying of Lady Catherine. Her claim to be a gentleman's daughter also fulfils Austen's requirement for a happy marriage: that the two parties should be socially compatible. It also reminds us that she has previously accused

Darcy of ungentlemanly behaviour, and that therefore it is manners which confer social status, not wealth.

> **'For what do we live, but to make sport for our neighbours, and laugh at them in our turn?' (pp. 343–44, Mr Bennet to Elizabeth)**

9

Although Mr Bennet provides much of the humour in the novel through his wit, he is also intelligent, unlike his wife or his cousin. He should therefore be capable of taking serious things seriously, particularly the choice of marriage partners for his daughters. Wisdom is better than wit, as Austen believed, and Mr Bennet fails in his responsibilities as both a husband and a father in his self-indulgent behaviour throughout the novel.

> **'As a child I was taught what was *right*, but I was not taught to correct my temper. I was given good principles, but left to follow them in pride and conceit.' (p. 349, Darcy to Elizabeth)**

10

Education and upbringing are important themes in this and every Austen novel, which use the traditions of Romance and the concept of the 'orphaned' child who has missing, unsuitable or morally defective parents. The heroes and heroines are forced to establish, through experience and by trial and error, their own values. Darcy and Elizabeth both have to learn to overcome their inadequate upbringing: indulgence in the former case, and negligence in the latter. For Austen love involved teaching, and Darcy and Elizabeth teach each other humiliating but beneficial lessons which cement their relationship.

Taking it further

Books

- Butler, M. (1988) *Jane Austen and the War of Ideas*, Clarendon Press.
- Cecil, D. (2000) *A Portrait of Jane Austen*, Penguin.
- Copeland, E. and McMaster, J. (eds) (1997) *The Cambridge Companion to Jane Austen*, Cambridge University Press.
- Gilbert, S. and Gubar, S. (2000) *The Madwoman in the Attic*, second edition, Yale University Press.
- Lascelles, M. (1995) *Jane Austen and her Art*, Continuum.
- Page, N. (1972) *The Language of Jane Austen*, Oxford University Press.
- Southam, B. (ed.) (1995) *Jane Austen: the Critical Heritage Vols 1 & 2*, Routledge.

- Southam, B. (ed.) (1976) *Jane Austen*: Sense and Sensibility, Pride and Prejudice *and* Mansfield Park: *A Casebook*, Palgrave Macmillan.
- Tomalin, C. (2000) *Jane Austen: A Life*, Penguin.
- Watt, I. (ed.) (1963) *Jane Austen: Twentieth Century Views*, Prentice Hall.

Film and television

All of the productions listed below are available on DVD from Amazon UK.

- **1940**: film version directed by Robert Z. Leonard, starring Greer Garson and Laurence Olivier, adapted by Aldous Huxley. Greer Garson claimed that the costumes were recycled from *Gone with the Wind* and therefore completely anachronistic. In this version Lady Catherine eventually agrees to the marriage. Slapstick comic scenes are inserted.
- **1980**: television series directed by Cyril Coke, starring Elizabeth Garvie and David Rintoul, adapted by Fay Weldon.
- **1995**: television series directed by Matthew Langton, starring Jennifer Ehle and Colin Firth, adapted by Andrew Davies. This was the celebrated production in which Colin Firth scandalised some 'Janeites' by emerging from the Pemberley lake in a wet shirt and tight white breeches.
- **2004**: 'Bollywood' version *Bride & Prejudice*, directed by Gurinder Chadha, starring Aishwarya Rai, Martin Henderson and Daniel Gillies, with the action transferred to present-day India.
- **2005**: film version directed by Joe Wright, starring Keira Knightley and Matthew Macfadyen, adapted by Deborah Moggach; many viewers consider the approach to be too modern, and Keira Knightley to be too pretty.

There are 11,500 clips from film and television productions of *Pride and Prejudice* to be found on Youtube (**www.youtube.com**) — just search for *Pride and Prejudice*.

Internet

An internet search for 'Pride and Prejudice' returns over 3,500,000 results. It would be more than a lifetime's work to go through all these; what follows is a selection of sites that are useful and seem to have broadly reliable information.

- **www.pemberley.com** The best site for all Jane Austen's work. This site has many useful features and links, including:
- **www.pemberley.com/janeinfo/pridprej.html** An illustrated and annotated hypertext of the novel.

- **www.gutenberg.org/etext/1342** Other full (searchable) e-texts of the novel from Project Gutenberg or from:
- **www.onlineliterature.com/austen/prideprejudice/**
- **www.shmoop.com/pride-and-prejudice/** Shmoop is a recently introduced site which includes a study guide and contributions from tutors at leading US universities.
- **www.jasna.org/** The Jane Austen Society of North America publishes this excellent website with an online journal, *Persuasions*, dealing with all of Austen's works.

Sequels

An extraordinary feature of the Jane Austen phenomenon is the large number of works of fiction, in prose, verse and drama, inspired by her novels and parasitic upon them. There are more than 20 sequels, prequels and alternative renderings of *Pride and Prejudice*, some by recognised novelists; perhaps the most prestigious is *Pemberley* by Emma Tennant (1993). At least eight have been published since 2002, so the trend shows no sign of abating.

- **www.erasofelegance.com/arts/literature/janebooks.html** This site offers a reasonably full list of such titles, with discussion.

---

*Pause for **Thought***

Why do you think so many sequels to *Pride and Prejudice* have been written? Is it a strength or a weakness of the book that readers wish to continue it?

---

*TASK **26***

Sketch your own continuation of the novel after the marriage of Elizabeth and Darcy. Make sure that what you propose is consistent with their characters as revealed in the novel. Write the first chapter in a way which reflects aspects of Austen's form, structure and language.